A GOOD FOOD DAY

Reboot Your
Health with Food
That Tastes Great

MARCO CANORA

WITH **TAMMY WALKER**

PHOTOGRAPHS BY MICHAEL HARLAN TURKELL

CLARKSON POTTER/PUBLISHERS
NEW YORK

Published in the United States by Clarkson Potter/Publishers,
an imprint of the Crown Publishing Group, a division of
Random House LLC, New York, a Penguin Random House
Company.
www.crownpublishing.com
www.clarksonpotter.com

CLARKSON POTTER is a trademark and POTTER with
colophon is a registered trademark of Random House LLC.

Library of Congress Cataloging-in-Publication Data
Canora, Marco.
  A good food day: reboot your health with food that tastes good
health/Marco Canora, with Tammy Walker; photographs by
Michael Harlan Turkell. —First edition.

  Includes bibliographical references and index.
  1. Cooking, American. 2. Natural foods. 3. Diet therapy.
  4. Nutrition. I. Walker, Tammy II. Title.
  TX715.C219 2014
  641.5973—dc23   2013050632

ISBN 978-0-385-34491-3
eISBN 978-0-385-34492-0

Printed in China

Interior and cover design by Rae Ann Spitzenberger
Cover photography by Michael Harlan Turkell

10 9 8 7 6 5 4 3 2 1

First Edition

TO MY WIFE, AMANDA,
AND OUR TWO BEAUTIFUL DAUGHTERS,
STELLA AND ZADIE

CONTENTS

FOREWORD

I vividly remember my first visit to 403 East 12 Street. As soon as I stepped in the door, I was met with curious questions.

The first was: "It's really assy, right?"

"Grassy?" I asked.

"No . . . assy," Marco repeated loudly, over the bustle of the bar.

It was true. The red wine that Marco had handed me smelled just like a barn. The hints of wet horse ass were unmistakable. This excited me because (a) the Chinon (Bernard Baudry, 2010, Loire Valley) was the best cabernet franc I'd ever had, and (b) I'd finally found a wine descriptor I could understand.

Marco Canora, of course, is co-owner and executive chef of the James Beard Award–nominated Hearth, where we now stood, just inside the entrance. Prior to striking out on his own, he held various positions at Gramercy Tavern and the famed Cibreo in Florence, Italy. He was Tom Colicchio's right-hand man as the original chef of Craft restaurant, which won a James Beard Award for Best New Restaurant during his tenure.

By the end of the evening, I concluded what many others had: Hearth is the most underrated restaurant in all of New York City.

"Cooking is not hard. Cooking is *not* hard." Marco repeated this five times during our evening together. "I feel like I've pulled the wool over everyone's eyes as a 'successful chef in New York City.' Anyone could do this."

"C'mon," I said as I pointed to my vegetable salad, which was ethereal and juicy (not an adjective I use for salads), easily one of the best salads of my life.

He laughed and waved a hand dismissively. "People say, 'Oh my God! This is amazing!' Just dress it while the vegetables are warm—it all soaks in. Pour the oil on after the red wine vinegar, and add salt and pepper. Anyone could do this."

And that's the beauty of Marco. He can show you how to "pull the wool over everyone's eyes" in wonderful, ethical ways. Can simple food be elegant? Can delicious food be fast? Can a three-ingredient dish—slapped together in five minutes—taste like it took hours to make? Yes, and, believe it or not, it can all be good for you, even if it tastes like sin.

I was introduced to Marco in 2009 because he'd lost 25-plus pounds experimenting with the Slow-Carb Diet® as described in *The 4-Hour Body*. He'd tweaked and fine-tuned the guidelines to complement his incredible culinary skills. It was a formidable combination . . . and a delicious one. He went from a size 40 waist to a size 35 waist without ever being hungry or bored.

But Marco's not rigidly dedicated to one "diet," per se.

Marco has cherry-picked his favorite aspects of many books over the years, testing it all in his kitchen and—more important—with

his stomach. He's added his own inventions, turned a few things upside down, put a twist on the classics, and created what you now hold in your hands: a guide to making masterpieces without being a master.

Marco is a pioneer, and I'll recommend that you follow in his footsteps. In the wise words of Bruce Lee: "Absorb what is useful, discard what is not, add what is uniquely your own."

You are in great hands. Enjoy the ride.

Pura vida,

TIM FERRISS
author of *The 4-Hour Workweek,*
The 4-Hour Body, and *The 4-Hour Chef*

INTRODUCTION

My Daily Bread

I've been a professional chef and cook for twenty years, the last sixteen of them in New York City. I'm a lifer, and I love it. But being a chef means crazy hours and even crazier eating habits. There's no such thing as "listening to your body" when you're a chef in a professional kitchen in New York. Awareness of my health and eating habits did not possess an iota of my brain space.

This is what a typical day for me, a working chef, used to look like: I wake up at 10 a.m. and hit the coffee. I don't feel hungry for breakfast because I was out last night, after dinner service, eating and drinking with chef buddies until 2 a.m. Coffee is my sustenance until I get to the restaurant in the afternoon—and that's when I start in on the bread. Loads of fresh bread arrive daily, so I swipe a heel of bread and continue picking at it for a few hours. Now it's time for a cigarette. I started smoking at age nineteen, but never considered myself a hardcore smoker. As long as my first cigarette isn't until the late afternoon, I'm doing all right. So, it's now 4:30 p.m. and, if you've added it up, the only thing I've put in my body is the questionable trinity of coffee, bread, and cigarettes.

Staff gathers for family meal at 4:30 p.m., my first meal of the day. Family meal is meant to be cost-effective and fit for a crowd. It's delicious, but not exactly the stuff Dr. Oz is preaching about. We're talking a lot of meat—and not the local grass-fed variety, but the cheaper cuts loaded with fat, growth hormones, and antibiotics—or starch-heavy food like pasta and garlic bread. Vegetables? Maybe a small pile of lettuce as an afterthought, but not much beyond that.

Amped up by another cigarette and a final large cup of coffee, I head into service. Six hours of bright lights, heat, speed, and constant stimulation whiz by. Though I tasted dozens of bites and ingested a full dinner's worth of calories, it never feels like they add up to a meal. Service winds down, and I'm thinking about relaxing with a smoke and a drink. After a few of each, I start to get hungry. I ate lunch at 4:30 p.m., so now that it's 1 a.m., I'm ready for dinner. It's how plenty of people feel when they finish their day of work, but for most it's 6 p.m., and for me and the rest of the working chefs it's 1 a.m.

At this hour, I'm not going home and whipping up a salad. I head to Corner Bistro for a few beers topped off by a cheeseburger, or go to Great New York Noodletown for a late-night Chinese feast of roast baby pig. On the nights I don't go out, I stop by the 24-hour bodega, order ham and cheese on a hard roll with mustard and watery lettuce, smash some potato chips in it, and nail that for my 1:30 a.m. dinner just before bed. I also make up for skipping the morning cigarettes by smoking ten in the last three hours of my night.

Remarkably, this was my routine for nearly twenty years. I was overcaffeinated, dehydrated, overstimulated, and full of starch, sugar, fatty meat, alcohol, and nicotine. Until my body started to stage a revolt.

Quite the glowing setup for a book on healthy eating, isn't it? As we all know, life has a way of kicking you in the ass. Being forced to make a significant shift in my own diet forced me to rethink what it means to cook and eat healthy. You'll be happy to know that it sure as hell doesn't mean deprivation or bland, pathetic-looking steamed vegetables. Eating nutritious foods that support feeling good isn't enough—these foods should satiate you and taste so good that you look forward to eating them. With the right arsenal of recipes, a healthy diet can coexist with delicious food. That's a good food day. My wife, Amanda, came up with the name for this concept, and it has steered my everyday eating habits for the past three years.

Now at forty-five, post-brink-of-disaster realization, I'm the healthiest I've ever been. I have loads of energy, I work out and practice yoga regularly, and I cook food that actually makes me excited to eat the way we know we're supposed to be eating. It's a complete U-turn from just four years ago, when I was a champ at treating my body like a piece of shit.

An Exercise in Futility

Here's a bit of irony for you: I grew up eating healthy whole foods. My after-school snack was a basket of mixed nuts, left in their shells with a nutcracker on the side. No sodas, no Ho Hos, no processed crap. My mom was far ahead of the curve in recognizing the importance of natural food. She was born and raised in Tuscany, where good food is central to everyday life, and much of it comes from the land just outside the kitchen window. So, while everyone else was grooving on breakfast cereals and bologna on white bread, my sister and I were eating frittatas with zucchini and basil, or warm string bean and potato salad, all made with fresh vegetables from the garden and dressed with good olive oil and red wine vinegar. I carry this with me in my own restaurant, Hearth, where I'm fanatical about preparing the absolute best-quality ingredients for our guests. When it came to feeding myself, though, my only requirement was that it be delicious. And for me, like many people in this country, "delicious" too often equates with sugar-laden, fatty, processed gut-bomb food.

The real kicker is I never thought about how what I ate might affect me in the future. I figured the physical requirements of my seventy-hour-a-week job made up for any excesses in my diet. It was my life. You weren't going to find me sweating it out at the gym or on the ball field—I was hunched over a cutting board.

When I hit my early thirties, I was diagnosed with sleep apnea and told that it would likely improve if I dropped some weight. This motivated me to start exercising, but it was only a half-assed effort until I was about thirty-seven. By then, Amanda and I had our daughter Stella, so I was over the late-night partying, but I was still smoking. My pants size had crept up from a 32 to a 38. I felt flabby and sluggish, but I thought exercise was the root of my weight issues. So I got a gym membership and, eventually, a personal trainer. That trainer was the first person to fill my head with solid nutrition advice—eating breakfast, switching to lean meats, putting vegetables back in my diet, etc.—but I still didn't change what I ate. I thought by working my ass off at the gym three days a week racking up hours of cardio, and cutting down on the late-night food fests, that the slim and trim Marco would appear.

But he didn't. I had more muscle definition, but I was still busting out of my pants and feeling bone-crushingly tired in the afternoon. And yeah, I was forty, and I knew things slow down as you get older, but I thought I had made every effort to see real results. What the hell?

Immensely frustrated and game for any help, I visited a nutritionist who came highly recommended by a couple of friends. I explained to him how I'd become a loyal gym rat but I'm not losing any weight, and how I feel completely sapped of energy, even though I'm sleeping through the night. I'm thinking the guy is going to give me a few helpful tweaks to my eating habits, and I'll be on my way.

Instead, he scared the shit out of me with cold, hard numbers: the results of my blood work and his evaluation. The verdict: I was pre-diabetic with blood glucose levels through the roof, I had seriously high cholesterol, and I was in the throes of full-blown gout—a painful form of inflammatory arthritis. I was also thirty pounds overweight and living on carbs, and my thyroid wasn't functioning properly. Not pretty. My nutritionist gave me lists of foods to avoid—one for my heightened cholesterol, one for my high blood sugar, and one for gout.

This humbling moment gave way to a hole of despair that I wallowed in for days. The news

My lovely wife, Amanda Filley. Without her, I'd still be an unhealthy wreck.

was terrifying. Don't get me wrong; I realize my condition could have been much, much worse. But the most alarming part wasn't my condition; it was the paralyzing thought that I couldn't enjoy food anymore. At the time, it seemed like I would be subjected to a life of calorie counting and eating celery sticks and unsalted almonds.

Food is the center of everything for me: my heritage, family, social life, and entire career. In short, it's a key player in my overall happiness. For just about anyone, the thought of overhauling your whole diet is a tough blow, but for me it fell just short of cruel. My diagnosis lit a fire under my ass to make some changes, but I knew I would be a miserable person and unable to stick to a healthy diet if I had to eat rabbit food for the rest of my life.

The Pleasure Factor

Once I got over my pity party, I launched into an all-out examination of what it means to have a healthy diet. Lucky for me, Amanda is incredibly well-read on nutrition and became my source of day-to-day guidance, introducing me to things like chia seeds, quinoa, and bee pollen and inspiring me to dig further into the nuts and bolts of how certain foods affected my body. To this day, she is a huge part of the reason I've become so interested in what it means to eat well. I dove into books on health and nutrition, absorbing everything I could from Gary Taubes, Dr. Alejandro Junger, Michael Pollan, Tim Ferriss, Robert Lustig, and Dr. Mark Hyman, among many others. It became somewhat of an obsession.

Every book has its own specific theories, but their collective advice all boils down to the same core messages about cutting down on sugar and processed foods, eating breakfast, and getting in more vegetables. The bummer is that without good recipes that deliver nutrition and delicious flavor, most of these books aren't exactly motivating anyone to step away from the bag of potato chips. Doctors, nutritionists, and foodie intellectuals offer a bounty of indispensable information, but knowing the techniques for making lean meats insanely flavorful or how to treat kale so it's crave-worthy isn't their forte. Judging by many of the recipes I came across, healthy cooking and eating were simply acts of necessity, not pleasure. Food as fuel, not joy. It's a message I could never wrap my head around.

Thankfully, I didn't have to rely on them for guidance in the kitchen. As a chef, I know

My two amazing daughters, Stella, 8, and Zadie, 2.

about proper seasoning and which ingredients deliver the best possible flavors to make a dish worth eating again and again. I also have a well-tuned palate and a sense of creativity and know-how in the kitchen. So, I got busy using my skills to create a stable of healthy ingredient–focused recipes that not only taste damn good but also embody my deep-rooted love and appreciation for great food.

With these 125 recipes, I've translated the advice on how you should eat into what you can cook: dishes that are delicious and satisfying, and that actually inspire you to want healthy foods at every meal. I'll help you take the basic tenets of a healthy diet and put them into action in your kitchen, so you're making good-for-you food you actually want to eat. I'm not a dietician, a doctor, or your mom. I'm not here to promote weight loss or low-carb, grain-free, low-fat, or no-meat diets or to ask you to play some numbers game with calories. My recipes are focused on whole, real foods that are nutritional powerhouses. This can include whole milk from a local dairy farm, or organic grass-fed beef, because both foods are natural and packed with nutrients. The idea of low-fat string cheese and 100-calorie cookie packs as healthy foods is total bullshit—those are processed foods, not *real* foods. Throughout the book, I'll share basic information about the nutrition topics that now influence my food choices, and you'll see how my recipes gibe with the principles of a good food day.

Like my first book, *Salt to Taste*, this collection of recipes is for everyday cooking. You won't find a laundry list of stuff you've never heard of, and you don't need to spend five hours in the kitchen. I take on the simplest of ingredients, the workhorses of healthy diets, and give you luscious flavor combinations and easy techniques that are designed for convenience and flexibility. Once you get into a groove, I hope you'll keep experimenting. Think of my recipes as a basic formula: Learn them, and then plug in the foods and flavors that speak to you. I'm not here to show you what a chef-genius I am—I want to share the most important and basic knowledge that will empower you to begin cooking delicious, nutritious food for yourself.

There's an evolution that happens when you decide to go down this road. Your will to live a healthier lifestyle starts to feed on itself. It becomes reflex. I was jazzed by the positive effects, like having more energy, shedding weight, and becoming a healthier role model for my daughters. When I eat an avocado salad, I get the same burst of pleasure and sense of indulgence that I used to get from inhaling a bacon cheeseburger. I'm not kidding or exaggerating. That's not to say I don't go for the occasional burger or slice of pizza—I do, and I go at it with gusto. But the change hits home when you have that late-night piece of cheesecake and realize that you no longer feel guilty about it because it's truly a treat, not a daily habit anymore.

If you recently decided to clean up your diet and you're afraid that any enjoyment of food is now out the window, or if you're already a healthy food pro and feel stuck in a cooking rut, you picked up the right book. With my recipes, you'll find that healthy eating doesn't mean being banished to a life of uninspired, bland chicken breasts and steamed broccoli. As a chef and healthy eater who knows and loves food and cooking, I'll show you that with a healthy diet, there is still joy in eating. A good food day isn't about patting yourself begrudgingly on the back for eating the way you're "supposed to," it's about eating super delicious food with a clear direction toward better health. My joy is derived first and foremost from food that tastes good, but the bonus is that now, it makes me feel good too.

10 PRINCIPLES FOR A GOOD FOOD DAY

It's easy to get bogged down in the constantly evolving, sometimes confusing details of healthy eating advice. The following set of principles is my stripped-down version of all the nutrition noise, and it functions as my day-to-day guide. There's no one-size-fits-all approach to a good food day, and your own definition of it may change over time. My hope is that this roadmap is flexible enough to help guide you, no matter what your interpretation.

1 Eating must be enjoyable. On a good food day, eating is still a primary source of pleasure. With quality ingredients, a few basic cooking skills, and the recipes in this book, you can create meals that are so delicious and satisfying, they feel indulgent. Deprivation isn't the solution—satisfaction is.

2 Cooking empowers you to eat better. By cooking your own food, you're in control of what goes in your body, and you won't eat nearly as much sugar, salt, and fat as what you'll get with processed foods. As Michael Pollan said, "Cooking, transforming the raw stuff of nature into nutritious and appealing things for us to eat and drink, is one of the interesting and worthwhile things we humans do."

3 Proper prior planning prevents piss-poor performance. Feeding yourself (and others) the right foods requires thought and planning. You don't want to have to cook every time you need to eat, so plan to make larger batches of leftover-friendly foods that can be repurposed into new meals. Many of the recipes in this book are scaled up for great leftovers—these will save you from a lot of poor impulse choices. It might seem overly time-consuming at first, but once you establish a system—planning meals, choosing a shopping day, and making a schedule for cooking days—it becomes a reflex.

4 Get in sync with Mother Nature. In-season ingredients check every important box: They are better tasting, more nutritious, higher quality, and more affordable. As seasons and ingredients shift, so should your cooking methods. You don't want a slow-cooked stew on a hot summer day or a cold tomato salad in the dead of winter, right?

5 **Quality ingredients are everything.** The closer a food is to its whole form, the better. The surest path to finding quality ingredients is your local farmers' market, where everything is fresh and in season. At a supermarket, organic becomes more of a priority because certified organic foods are held to a higher standard of production. Choose the highest-quality option you can afford.

6 **Eat real food.** Many processed foods have artificial ingredients, chemicals, additives, and excess salt, sugar, and potentially harmful types of fat. This can be true even if the food is organic or from a health food store, or screams buzzwords like "whole grain!" on the package. If you buy processed foods, ignore the labels and let the ingredient list be your guide. Look for real ingredients that you know are good for you.

7 **Be a conscious eater.** The act of eating should be a restorative interlude in your stressful, chaotic day, not a time for multitasking. By giving meals the attention they deserve, you eat at a slower pace and give your body a chance to register taste and satisfaction. You wind up feeling satiated with smaller portion sizes and enjoying your food more. Slow down. Chew. Savor your food.

8 **A twinge of hunger isn't the end of the world.** Most of us shovel food down with such frequency that we don't know what hungry feels like. Familiarizing yourself with hunger signals is a key part of learning to feed yourself well. Not shaky, lightheaded, desperation hunger, but the twinge of tightening in your stomach that first alerts you to hunger. When you start from this point, you'll discover which foods and quantities truly satisfy you. You may need a lot less food than you think.

9 **Diversify.** Food boredom is frustrating and leads back to old habits and crappy choices. Eating well for the long term requires choosing foods with a wide range of flavors, colors, and textures. This not only keeps meals interesting and satisfying, but eating a variety of foods also increases your chances of getting all the nutrients you need.

10 **Make indulgences a guilt-free part of the program.** Call it a cheat day, the 90/10 rule (eat well 90 percent of the time, splurge the other 10 percent), or whatever resonates with you. Granting yourself permission to say "to hell with it" once in a while increases your chances of successfully sticking to good eating habits.

PANTRY STAPLES FOR A GOOD FOOD DAY

To stack the odds in favor of having a good food day, it's essential to surround yourself with the right foods—those that really amp up the flavor *and* the nutrition of your meals. This list is a window into my kitchen on an average week. It's by no means exhaustive, since much of my cooking is driven by seasonal produce and fresh fish and meat. But you'll find most of the ingredients you need to prepare the recipes in this book, plus a few other basics that lend themselves to easy, delicious impromptu meals and keep you out of the fast-food drive-thru line. The good-for-you benefits of many of the items here are covered within the chapters where I put them into action, so this list is an at-a-glance shopping reference. Also, I don't call out local or organic in front of every food here—these are a given for me (see Principle #5), and a personal choice based on your budget.

You might raise an eyebrow at a few items here, but each has its place in a healthy diet. Right off the bat, you can see I don't shy away from fat. Good fats, even some saturated fats like whole milk and grass-fed butter, are foundation ingredients in every one of my recipes for flavor, mouthfeel, and, yes, their nutrition benefits (see page 22). I also don't think there's anything inherently wrong with eating meat, as long as it's properly sourced. So, even though they're often associated with healthy eating, I don't use meat substitutes like tofu, tempeh, or seitan. It boils down to this—taking a whole food in its natural form and processing it (to remove its fat, reduce its carbs, or turn it into something that acts like meat) denatures it to some degree. Processed foods are never as good as the real deal.

FRESH AND IN THE FRIDGE

Dairy

- Whole milk
- Unsweetened almond milk, rice milk, and hemp milk
- Full-fat plain yogurt—Greek and regular
- Grass-fed butter
- Cheese, glorious cheese—Parmigiano-Reggiano, Pecorino Romano, cheddar, and goat cheese or Gouda

Animal proteins

- Eggs
- Grass-fed ground beef
- Poultry—thighs, boneless skinless breasts, and whole
- Fish—wild Alaskan salmon, local white fish, olive oil–packed brown anchovies in a jar for cooking, and marinated white anchovies for using whole

Produce

- Fresh lemons, limes, bananas, and whatever fruit is in season
- For everyday cooking—red and yellow onions, garlic, carrots, celery, avocado, fresh ginger, and any in-season vegetables
- Hardy cooking greens—Tuscan kale, Swiss chard, escarole, spinach, cabbage, and bok choy
- Salad greens—arugula, dandelion, red leaf lettuce, and Bibb lettuce

Raw nuts and seeds

(yes, these should be refrigerated, so they stay fresh longer)

- Seeds—chia, flax, pumpkin, and sunflower
- Nuts—almonds, walnuts, pistachios, hazelnuts, pine nuts, and pecans
- Almond butter, raw and unsalted
- Peanut butter, unsweetened

Stocks

- Chicken, vegetable, and mushroom

Flours and nut meals

(refrigerate; otherwise they'll go rancid)

- Flours—whole wheat, spelt, rye, buckwheat,* corn (flour, not meal), coconut, oat,* millet, and chickpea
- Nut meals*—almond and hazelnut

*These flours and nut meals can be made by grinding the whole grain or nut in a food processor.

Condiments

- Dijon mustard and whole-grain mustard
- Lacto-fermented vegetables
- Soy sauce, tamari, fish sauce
- Olives—niçoise and Castelvetrano
- Capers in brine

IN THE FREEZER

- Vegetables—carrots, broccoli, spinach, peas, and string beans
- Fruit—blueberries, blackberries, raspberries, and bananas (peeled and frozen for smoothies)
- Breads—Food for Life Ezekiel 4:9 Sprouted Whole Grain Bread and Nordic Breads Finnish Ruis

IN THE PANTRY

Oils and vinegars

- Extra virgin olive oil
- Virgin coconut oil
- Nut and seed oils—walnut oil, hazelnut oil, and sesame oil (cold-pressed)
- Vinegars—red wine, white wine, balsamic, apple cider, sherry, rice, brown rice

Canned goods

- Tomato paste
- Whole peeled tomatoes
- Unsweetened coconut milk

Dried beans and lentils

- Beans—cannellini, cranberry, pinto, black, kidney, and chickpeas
- Lentils—Puy and brown

Dried fruits

- Cranberries, raisins, dates, figs, and mango

Seasonings and spices

- Sea salt—fine-grain and large flake
- Whole black peppercorns—preground pepper does not come close to the flavor of whole peppercorns freshly ground in a pepper mill
- Whole spices—cinnamon sticks, cloves, star anise, fennel seeds, dried chile peppers, nutmeg
- Ground spices—cinnamon, ginger, coriander, cardamom, chili powder, za'atar, Chinese five-spice powder, curry powder, cayenne pepper, smoked paprika
- Whole vanilla beans and pure vanilla extract
- Dried rosemary and dried oregano
- Dried porcini and dried shiitake mushrooms
- Tea—green, ginger, and black
- Coffee

Whole grains

- Oats—rolled, steel-cut
- Buckwheat groats
- Rice—brown sweet and brown basmati
- Farro
- Freekeh
- Quinoa
- Amaranth
- Millet
- Barley
- Bulgur wheat

Sweeteners

- Maple syrup
- Honey—raw honey, clover (light) and buckwheat or chestnut (dark)
- Coconut palm sugar
- Unsulfured blackstrap molasses
- Light brown sugar

Chocolate

- Unsweetened raw cacao powder
- Dark chocolate (70% cacao or higher)

THE BIG FAT MYTH

More than a few questionable trends were born in the '80s (acid-wash jeans, sun-dried tomatoes, my smoking habit), and one of the more notorious still lives on today—fat phobia. For years, the U.S. Department of Agriculture (USDA) has handed us the line that fat is evil, especially saturated fat, and that it turns you into a blimp with high cholesterol and clogged arteries. People have traded fat-containing foods like steak, butter, and eggs for chemical-laden mutant foods. The fact is that while everyone was busy stressing over fat grams, we all got fatter. What gives? Well, we replaced fat with sugar and refined carbohydrates—the real culprits behind weight gain, diabetes, and heart disease. Fat brings flavor, so manufacturers made up for it by loading "healthy" fat-free foods with sugar. Like all refined carbs, sugar only increases your appetite, setting the stage for you to polish off a box of reduced-fat Snackwell cookies in one sitting (see page 250 for more on sugar's effects on the body).

We need fat, and the quality of fat is as important as the quantity. Natural mono-

unsaturated and polyunsaturated fats found in extra virgin olive oil, walnuts, salmon, flax-seeds, and avocados can improve blood cholesterol levels and reduce the risk for heart disease. I'm sure you've heard of omega-3 fatty acids, a class of polyunsaturated fats known for fighting inflammation, with such huge benefits that they get their own spotlight (page 56). Good fats make food more satisfying, so having a reasonable amount at every meal can keep you from packing on weight. Eating a piece of toast with mashed avocado curbs your hunger longer than toast with jelly, because the fat in avocado slows down the absorption of carbohydrates in the bread. Your blood sugar stays steadier, and you're less likely to be elbow-deep in a bag of snacks before your next meal. You also need good fats so your body can absorb more of the fat-soluble vitamins in vegetables, including vitamins D and E (yet another reason fat-free dressings are a bad idea—they do nothing to help you absorb all the good your salads can do).

The bad fats, so we've been told for decades, are the saturated fats in meat, butter, cheese, dark chocolate, and coconut. These fats are supposedly responsible for our high cholesterol, heart attacks, and strokes—but this is just plain wrong. The demonization of saturated fat can be traced back to one scientist, Ancel Keys, and his flawed Seven Countries Study that began in the 1950s. Keys's study compared fat intake and heart disease in seven countries and found those that ate the most fat had the highest rates of heart disease. The sketchy part? Keys gathered statistics for twenty-two countries, but focused only on the seven that supported his theory that saturated fat contributes to heart disease. If every country studied had been included, the results would show that there was no link. Unfortunately, Keys's version of the results took hold, the medical community and our government started recommending a low-fat diet, and people loaded up on fat-free frozen waffles and I Can't Believe It's Not Butter.

As I write this, there's still no large-scale study showing saturated fat leads to a higher risk of heart disease. This doesn't mean it's as beneficial as unsaturated fat, but we know some types of saturated fats are harmless, and others have proven to be helpful. We now know that stearic acid, one of the saturated fats in beef and the main one in dark chocolate, raises HDL (good) cholesterol and has no effect on LDL (bad) cholesterol, and that the lauric acid in virgin coconut oil improves overall cholesterol levels. Keep this in mind when you see butter, whole milk, and beef in a handful of my recipes—you may balk at these saturated fats as part of a healthy diet, but they do, in fact, have a rightful place when they come from a quality source.

The undisputed villains are artificial trans fats, used to increase the shelf life of processed foods like cake mixes, soups, frosting, pastries, and chips. They're also in the partially hydrogenated oil used for frying at most fast-food joints. Trans fats raise levels of LDL cholesterol and lower those of HDL cholesterol, and have been linked to the extra rolls of belly fat people carry around. Food manufacturers are now required to list the amount of trans fats, so many of them changed their formulas to cut down. But they're still lurking, thanks to a loophole that allows foods with up to 0.5 grams of trans fat per serving to be listed as zero. Even though the Food and Drug Administration is making moves to eliminate artificial trans fats entirely, the easiest way to avoid them is to lay off processed foods entirely. Check ingredient lists for "partially hydrogenated oil" or "hydrogenated oil"—the giveaway that trans fats are present.

I also stay away from vegetable oils like canola, corn, and soybean. Sure, they're unsaturated and have some omega-3s, but unlike extra virgin olive oil, they can't be extracted through pressing naturally. They're heavily processed, overheated, and deodorized, all of which involves potentially harmful chemicals. It's mind-boggling to me that these are recommended as healthy when their processing requires the same solvent (hexane) that's used in shoe glue.

Good fats have to be key players in everything I eat. Extra virgin olive oil has always been a given in my cooking, but I've branched out, adding full-fat Greek yogurt and almond butter to breakfast shakes, coconut milk to soups and desserts, chia seeds to oatmeal and snacks. They make food delicious and satisfying—and replacing a lot of refined carbs and sugar with good fats is ultimately how I lost and now maintain my weight. Repeat after me: Good fat does *not* make you fat!

BREAKFAST

I'VE SPENT MY ENTIRE LIFE NOT being hungry in the morning. I hear the same tune from other people too: "Why should I eat breakfast if I'm not hungry?" The better question to ask is "Why am I *not* hungry?" The answer is probably because you ate too much or too late the night before. That was certainly the case for me during all those years when I lulled myself into a food coma with a plate of pork and a half dozen beers at 1 a.m.

Advice on healthy eating can be conflicting as hell, but there is one key nugget that is nearly undisputed: the importance of eating breakfast. Take the word *breakfast* at face value: The meal is meant to "break the fast" you've been in while sleeping. It kicks your metabolism into gear, lessening your likelihood of turning into a ravenous pig later in the day. A slew of studies also show that eating breakfast increases mental clarity and the overall ability to get shit done.

Given the load of evidence that eating breakfast is a cornerstone of a healthy diet, I trained myself to be hungry in the morning by not eating after 9 p.m. This cuts out all the mindless munching and late-night meals that get in the way of restorative sleep and the desire to eat after waking up. It may mean that you occasionally go to bed with a twinge of hunger—that's okay. Our ancestors didn't have round-the-clock access to food like we do. We are built to get by without midnight snacks. The "kitchen-closed" time may be different for you based on your schedule, but if you stop eating 12 hours before you plan to wake up—and you do this diligently—you'll get to know morning hunger.

All breakfasts are not created equal, so choosing the right foods in the right quantity is crucial. In the typical American diet, the day starts with a big bowl of cereal or a sugary pastry the size of your head. Low in protein and fiber, these breakfasts are nothing but simple carbohydrates that leave you feeling limp and hungry two hours later. I'm willing to bet that if you need a snack to make it to lunchtime, you've got a simple carb situation going on at breakfast. You need foods with staying power, so the recipes in this chapter favor protein, fiber, and quality fats, using eggs, nuts, fruits, and whole grains, foods containing nutrients that take more time for your body to digest. They hang out in your stomach for a while, making you feel fuller longer and giving you a more steady supply of energy.

Besides not feeling hungry in the morning, the biggest rant I hear about breakfast is that there's no time for it. I get that—I'm on autopilot in the morning, and on a weekday I don't want to think about what to make while rubbing the sleep out of my eyes. Breakfast should be a no-brainer, and speed is the name of the game, so keeping pantry staples stocked and having on-the-fly breakfast ideas like those here are of major importance.

Most of us are creatures of habit when it comes to breakfast. I get hooked on a particular kind of breakfast and try a million and one varieties. I did that with shakes (a great starting point if you're not used to eating breakfast), then cycled into an egg kick, and now I'm in a breakfast sandwich phase. This chapter holds all my favorites— the ones that consistently lure me out of bed. A few are make-ahead recipes that I keep around for especially comatose or rushed mornings. Others come together quickly thanks to staples like frozen fruit, eggs, oats, and whole-grain bread. I've also included options for those days when you have the luxury of time and want something special.

Whatever you do, don't skip breakfast. It's not a good food day without it.

DARK BERRY SHAKE MAKES 1 SHAKE

In the summer, I use fresh berries from the greenmarket, but the rest of the time I use frozen organic berries. I love how the frozen berries make the shake extra frothy. Ground ginger is one of my go-to breakfast spices, along with cinnamon. The ginger works especially well in fruit shakes where it's a nice, subtle kick alongside the fruit's natural sugars. ∎

Berries have the highest antioxidant levels of any other commonly available fruit. Antioxidants are disease-fighting powerhouses that protect the body against the effects of aging and may help prevent heart disease and certain types of cancer. Berries are also high in fiber and vitamins C and E. When these gems aren't in season, hit the freezer section—frozen berries have the same nutritional jackpot as fresh.

½ cup blueberries

½ cup blackberries

¼ cup full-fat plain Greek yogurt

¾ cup unsweetened almond milk

1 tablespoon virgin coconut oil

½ teaspoon ground ginger

1 tablespoon chia seeds

Add everything to a blender and buzz until smooth, about 1 minute.

MANGO GREEN SHAKE **MAKES 1 SHAKE**

Green juices continue to be the darlings of the healthy food world, but there are plenty out there that are primarily fruit juice packed with sugar and only a couple of green leaves. Hardly the veggie-centric health tonic you expect it to be. I prefer green shakes, because using whole fruits and vegetables slows down the body's blood sugar response, and the fiber means you feel full sooner and longer. In this reviving shake, creamy, sweet mango meets refreshing cucumber and coconut water, along with an unexpected green: cilantro. The word is that eating cilantro is a natural way to cleanse your body of heavy metals like mercury and lead. As a former smoker, I should probably be eating the stuff by the fistful. Cilantro: It's not just a garnish for tacos! ∎

½ cup frozen mango chunks

¼ cup lightly packed cilantro leaves

½ cucumber, sliced (about 1 cup)

¾ cup coconut water

Juice of 1 small lime

Add everything to a blender and buzz until smooth and creamy, about 1 minute.

CHOCOLATE SHAKE MAKES 1 SHAKE

Chocolate for breakfast. That's basically what's going on here. Thanks to raw, unsweetened organic cacao powder, you can start your day or feed a post-dinner sweet tooth with a decadent, disease-fighting shake. If you need a chocolate fix, this shake's deep, rich chocolate flavor does the job. The sweetness comes from the ripe banana, so if your bananas still have a green tint when you freeze them, you may want to add a teaspoon of honey to the shake. ∎

Unsweetened raw cacao powder is high in flavonoids, which are powerful antioxidants found in plants. When raw cacao beans are made into packaged chocolate products, the flavonoids and all their benefits are lost. So, your healthiest option is unsweetened organic raw cacao powder. Use it in this shake, stir it into oatmeal, bake with it, or make a killer hot chocolate.

1 ripe banana, peeled and frozen

1 tablespoon raw almond or cashew butter

2 tablespoons unsweetened raw cacao powder

1 cup unsweetened almond milk

½ teaspoon ground cinnamon

Add everything to a blender and buzz until smooth and creamy, about 1 minute.

SHAKES

The only shake I used to drink was one made from a half-quart of ice cream. Of course, a few hours later I was nursing a milkshake hangover (with some form of bread).

When I started creating the breakfast habit, my focus on high-protein options led me to protein powder, and a shake was the easiest way to use it. I've since moved away from protein powders, because I'm more into using whole foods to get my necessary nutrients. However, shakes still do it for me, especially in the spring and summer when something cold for breakfast seems like a good idea. I also love shakes because of the mobility factor: I'm usually pouring the contents of the blender into a glass jar and flying out the door.

My morning shake is the only time I'm okay with drinking my calories, because I know it's filled with quality whole foods. The protein comes from ingredients like almond butter, chia seeds, Greek yogurt, and oats. The liquid base varies, but it's typically almond milk—it's thinner than cow's milk, but it still has body; and its nutty flavor and faint sweetness work well in all kinds of shakes. The key to thick, creamy shakes isn't milk or ice cream—it's frozen bananas. I recommend cutting peeled bananas into chunks before freezing them, especially if you're not working with a high-powered blender. Frozen fruit in general is great for shakes because it adds flavor, fiber, and a frosty quality that eliminates the need for ice.

ODE TO ORANGE JULIUS SHAKE MAKES 1 SHAKE

Orange Julius stores were a huge part of mall culture in the '80s, and my teenage weekends of cruising the mall always included their sweet, frothy orange drinks. My play on the classic Julius is just as cold, creamy, and bright, but it's naturally sweetened and uses Greek yogurt to boost the protein factor. I also use whole fresh fruit, not just the juice, to add fiber and thickness. We send out a complimentary shot glass of this shake to brunch guests at Hearth. ∎

½ grapefruit, peeled

½ orange, peeled

½ teaspoon pure vanilla extract

1 tablespoon raw honey

1 cup ice

½ cup full-fat plain Greek yogurt

Add everything to a blender and buzz until smooth and creamy, about 1 minute.

Most commercial honey, like the kind in the squeezy bear bottles, is treated with a high heat process that destroys some of honey's natural vitamins, minerals, and enzymes. I prefer to use raw, unprocessed honey. It has not been heated or filtered so it still contains bee pollen and all of its beneficial nutrients. Raw honey looks different than processed versions—it's opaque and solid at room temperature. Buy it at your local farmer's market, and save it for recipes where it won't be heated, like this shake.

GOJI BERRY AND BANANA SHAKE MAKES 1 SHAKE

This filling shake skews sweet, so if you're trying to wean yourself off sugary cereals, give this one a go. Goji berries, the star of this bright orange-red shake, get a lot of buzz for their antioxidant powers. Here, their tangy sweetness is balanced by ground flaxseed, which adds a nutty flavor, good fat, and fiber. Don't skip soaking the goji berries; this plumps and softens them. If you don't have a minute to spare in the morning, soak them overnight. ∎

¼ cup dried goji berries, soaked in water for 10 minutes and drained

1 ripe banana, peeled and frozen

½ cup unsweetened rice milk

2 tablespoons ground flaxseed

½ cup ice

Add everything to a blender and buzz until smooth and creamy, about 1 minute. Give it a taste and add more rice milk or ice if you like a thinner shake.

Goji berries are commonly found in dried form and look like red raisins. Some of the goji berry hype is overblown and related to an ancient Chinese myth that they can cure anything and help you drastically extend your lifespan. But their crazy-high levels of beta carotene (which converts to vitamin A in the body) and vitamin C, and high concentration of protein (more than any other fruit), make them worth adding to your shakes or munching on as a snack.

PEAR-MAPLE
OATMEAL SHAKE MAKES 1 SHAKE

When you think of oatmeal, a beverage probably isn't among the first things that come to mind. It wasn't for me either until one sleepy morning when I was deciding between making a shake and grabbing some leftover steel-cut oats. I ended up with a mash-up of breakfasts that's reminiscent of a thick, creamy milkshake. It has all the fiber and staying power of steel-cut oats in the conveniently portable form of a shake. There's a slight chew to it, which helps signal a sense of fullness. Bartlett pears are sweet and juicy, the two characteristics you need to balance the heft of the oatmeal. The fall flavors of pear and maple are made to go together. ∎

¾ cup cooked, cooled Steel-Cut Oats (opposite)

1 Bartlett pear, chopped (about 1 cup)

½ cup unsweetened almond milk

1 tablespoon maple syrup

Add everything to a blender and buzz until completely smooth, about 1 minute. If you feel it's too thick, add a few extra tablespoons of almond milk to reach the consistency you like.

CHERRY-VANILLA
OATMEAL SHAKE MAKES 1 SHAKE

This shake was inspired by Ben & Jerry's Cherry Garcia, still one of the world's greatest ice cream flavors (and one I haven't had much of since I changed my eating habits). The cherries and vanilla are great on their own, but I occasionally toss in a little cacao powder for added richness. ∎

¾ cup cooked, cooled Steel-Cut Oats (opposite)

1 cup fresh or frozen pitted Bing cherries

¼ teaspoon pure vanilla extract

½ cup unsweetened almond milk

2 teaspoons unsweetened raw cacao powder (optional)

Add everything to a blender and buzz until completely smooth, about 1 minute. If you feel it's too thick, add a couple tablespoons of almond milk to reach the consistency you like.

POT OF STEEL-CUT OATS SERVES 6 TO 8

In the colder months, no other breakfast feels as hearty and fortifying, or keeps me satisfied as long as a bowl of hot steel-cut oats. There's an incredible nutty creaminess that happens when the starch releases from the oats and mingles with almond and coconut milks. Their cooking time isn't conducive to the morning rush, so we make a big batch in the evening and eat it for the next three or four days as a quick no-brainer breakfast. Steel-cut oats are chunkier than rolled oats and have a sturdy, chewy texture that holds up well to reheating (unlike rolled oats, which can get gluey). I find they're even better the next day, after having some time to sit with the milk and cinnamon. There are mornings when I dig in as is, but toppings help keep it interesting from day to day. My go-to combination is dried fruit with chopped hazelnuts and a tablespoon of maple syrup, but you can take it any direction you like with fruit, nuts, spices, and natural sweeteners. ■

Coconut milk is pressed from the meat of a coconut, which is a gold mine of nutritional value. It's high in a type of saturated fat that has germ- and disease-fighting powers and may help lower total cholesterol levels. Coconut milk's bounty also includes vitamins E and C, iron, calcium, potassium, and antioxidants galore. It's available in cartons and cans, and for cooking I prefer the thick, rich texture of canned coconut milk: When you pop open a can, the milk may look separated, but it just needs to be stirred. Coconut milk in a carton is thinner and more drinkable, but it usually comes sweetened or flavored with a handful of questionable additives.

Steel-cut oats, also called Irish oats, are chunky pieces of whole oat kernels (oat groats). These thick pieces take longer to digest and are lower on the glycemic index than rolled oats, which have to go through more processing to get their flat shape. Steel-cut oats have more protein than rolled oats, but both varieties have the same high level of fiber and are light-years better than the sugar-bomb packets of instant oats.

2 cups steel-cut oats

½ cup canned whole unsweetened coconut milk

½ cup unsweetened almond milk, plus more for serving

1 cinnamon stick

Large pinch of fine sea salt

1 In a large pot, combine all the ingredients with 4 cups water and bring to a boil. Reduce the heat to a simmer, cover, and cook for 15 minutes, stirring occasionally, until the oats are cooked through and creamy.

2 Transfer the cooked oats and cinnamon stick to a glass storage container and let them cool before storing in the fridge.

3 In the morning, portion out your oatmeal (I do about ¾ cup per serving) and heat it up on the stove with ¼ cup almond milk to thin it out a bit.

GLYCEMIC INDEX & GLYCEMIC LOAD

Why Slow and Low Is Best

Bread is my biggest weakness, and it used to be the first thing I ate every day. Whether it was an artisanal loaf or the cheap, sliced stuff, I was in. My craving for bread was matched only by a fierce love for pasta (heaven distilled into a food). I knew they weren't healthy foods, but I didn't know they were making me a blood-sugar train wreck. When I visited my doctor complaining of slothlike fatigue, he pointed out that I was eating too much white flour and sugar—refined carbs that have no fiber or nutrients. This caused my blood sugar to spike and then drastically dip, cueing exhaustion and cravings. My blood tests confirmed I was pre-diabetic, basically the last stop on the road to full-blown type 2 diabetes.

Had I learned about the Glycemic Index (GI) and Glycemic Load (GL) a lot sooner, I could have started choosing better-quality carbs. Carbohydrates are basically long chains of glucose (sugar) molecules, which your digestive system breaks down and releases into your bloodstream to be used for energy. By ranking how high and how quickly carbohydrate-containing foods raise your blood sugar level, both the GI and GL help you figure out the best carbs to eat and make it much easier to control your blood sugar, manage your weight, and keep your body humming along with a steady (rather than spiking) supply of energy.

The GI scale is 0 to 100: Foods under 55 are low GI, between 56 and 69 are medium, and above 70 are high. The higher the GI ranking, the quicker that food can send you into a wild sugar rush followed by an exhausting crash. You can easily pick those foods out of a lineup— white bread, white pasta, French fries, potato chips, soda, candy. When you regularly consume too many servings of high-GI foods like I did, you're more likely to pack on pounds and increase your risk of developing insulin resistance and type 2 diabetes (see page 250 for more on how this works). The lower a food's GI ranking, the longer it takes to break down in your gut, resulting in a slow-and-steady drip of glucose into your bloodstream. Choosing complex carbs with low GI—almost all vegetables, most fruits, and some beans and grains— is especially crucial at breakfast so you set off with a steady supply of energy for the day. These foods also tend to be higher in fiber, keeping you fuller longer.

By using the GI as a general guide, I started swapping in low-GI alternatives for my usual crew. I replaced refined and white flour breads with whole-grain breads, like the sourdough rye bread I use in the Breakfast Sandwiches (page 49). I chose nuts instead of potato chips, whole wheat pasta instead of white flour pasta. Simply by choosing lower-GI foods, I reversed my prediabetic state and came back to normal blood sugar levels in just a matter of months. (See the chart opposite, detailing the whole scale of the GI/GL index.)

But of course there are some head-scratchers within the index. The GI values for watermelon and carrots are high, and spaghetti has a lower GI than brown rice. This flies in the face of all

THE GLYCEMIC INDEX & GLYCEMIC LOAD VALUES

GI: Low is 1–55, medium is 56–69, and high is 70–100

GL: Low is 1–10, medium is 11–19, and high is 20 and above

FOOD	GI VALUE	GL VALUE
Grapefruit	25	3
Cashews	27	3
Chickpeas	28	8
Lentils	29	5
Apple	38	6
Whole milk	41	5
Grapes	46	8
Spaghetti	46	22
Orange	48	5
Brown rice	50	16
Banana	52	14
Quinoa	53	13
Steel-cut oats	55	13
Sweet corn	60	20
Sweet potato	61	17
White rice	64	23
Instant oatmeal	66	17
Cranberry juice	68	24
Watermelon	72	4
Popcorn	72	7
Cornflakes	81	21
Baked russet potato	85	26

common sense. The solution? The Glycemic Load, a relatively new measurement that factors in a key piece of information that the GI doesn't: the amount of carbohydrates in a realistic portion of the food. Let's use watermelon as an example. The carbohydrates in watermelon quickly turn into sugar, so it's high on the glycemic index at 72. But an average serving size of watermelon doesn't have many carbohydrates; you would have to practically gorge on the stuff to get a rapid rise in blood sugar. So thanks to the GL, foods like watermelon, carrots, and cantaloupe are cleared of their former bad-for-blood-sugar reputation. A GL of 10 or less is low, 11 to 19 is medium, 20 or more is high. In a real-life portion size of watermelon (½ cup), the GL value is 4, making it low glycemic.

Ultimately, both indexes are useful. The Glycemic Index helps you choose better-quality carbs, and the Glycemic Load guides you to reasonable portion sizes. I've found the best strategy is to use them together: familiarize yourself with where things fall on the scale and try to stick to mostly low- and medium-GI and GL foods, only dabbling in high. At breakfast, this means going for steel-cut oats (page 33) instead of instant oatmeal, muffins or pancakes made of whole-grain flour (pages 44 and 50) rather than white flour, and whole fruit instead of just fruit juice. A great reference for more information on the glycemic index and glycemic load is *The New Glucose Revolution* by Jennie Brand-Miller.

The most noticeable difference from my high-GI carb frenzy to now is my energy level. I'm no longer dragging around in a fog of exhaustion. My tastes have also changed—I now crave the nuttier whole-grain breads rather than whatever I can get my hands on. Before, I was caught in a loop of "I can't get no satisfaction" when it came to bread. Now, by keeping my blood sugar steady with the help of low-GI eating, I've realized a level of satisfaction from food that I was completely missing out on before.

NO-COOK OVERNIGHT OATS

If you need instant gratification in the morning, this is your breakfast (so no need to make a big batch as you would with the steel-cut oats). Before going to bed, take a minute to mix rolled oats with milk, chia seeds, a bit of cinnamon and ginger, and some mashed banana for natural sweetness. Overnight, the oats soften and absorb the milk, while the chia seeds work their gel-forming action to thicken the whole mixture. In the morning, you have a thick, voluminous bowl of lightly spiced and sweetened oats that are especially great cold or room temperature (though you can heat it up if cold oats aren't your thing). I think of it as a high-fiber, high-protein "summer porridge." Berries with sliced almonds or coconut flakes with almond butter are my favorite topping combos, but whatever fruit, nuts, or nut butter you like would be good. ■

Chia seeds are one of the health-nut ingredient trends that really live up to the hype. Native to Central America and Mexico, just 1 tablespoon of these small wonders delivers a healthy dose of complete protein, fiber, and omega-3 fatty acids. Chia seeds have a neutral flavor, so you can work them in anywhere.

½ cup old-fashioned rolled oats

1 tablespoon chia seeds

½ teaspoon ground cinnamon

¼ teaspoon ground ginger

Pinch of fine sea salt

1 cup unsweetened almond milk, plus a splash for serving

½ ripe banana, mashed

Fruits, nuts, or nut butter for serving

1 In a bowl, stir together the oats, chia seeds, cinnamon, ginger, and salt. Pour in the almond milk, and stir in the mashed banana. Refrigerate overnight.

2 In the morning, stir in a splash of almond milk to loosen things up and add whatever toppings you like.

HIGH-PROTEIN OVERNIGHT OATS SERVES 1

Stirring plain full-fat Greek yogurt into the overnight mixture makes for extra creamy oats with an additional dose of protein. To give it a chocolate pudding vibe, I'll occasionally stir a tablespoon of cacao powder into the overnight mixture. ∎

Both Greek yogurt and regular yogurt have probiotics, the good bacteria (the "live and active cultures" referred to on the package) that contribute to a healthy digestive system. Thanks to the longer straining and filtering process Greek yogurt goes through, it has less sugar and almost double the amount of protein. Not all Greek yogurts are created equal, though. Choose plain to avoid the addition of evaporated cane juice, which is hardly better than plain old white sugar.

½ cup old-fashioned rolled oats

1 tablespoon chia seeds

½ teaspoon ground cinnamon

¼ teaspoon ground ginger

Pinch of fine sea salt

⅔ cup unsweetened almond milk, plus a splash for serving

½ cup full-fat plain Greek yogurt

1½ teaspoons maple syrup or honey

Fruit, nuts, or nut butter, for serving

1 In a bowl, stir together the oats, chia seeds, cinnamon, ginger, and salt. Add the almond milk, yogurt, and maple syrup and stir until thoroughly combined. Refrigerate overnight.

2 In the morning, stir in a splash of almond milk to loosen things up and add whatever toppings you like.

BUCKWHEAT GROATS WITH APRICOTS AND ALMONDS SERVES 1

A hot, velvety porridge of buckwheat groats is a great alternative to oatmeal. It's prepared with the same basic process, but buckwheat has a more pronounced earthy, nutty flavor, and the triangle-shaped groats give the porridge a spectacular, chewy texture. Tossing in chia seeds adds a boost of fiber and healthy fats. Fresh apricots are best, but when they're not in season you can substitute dried apricots. When using dried, add them halfway through the groats cooking, so they have time to soften. ∎

Despite its grainlike tendencies, buckwheat is actually the seed of a plant similar to rhubarb, not a type of wheat. At the store, you'll find it in its hulled form as buckwheat groats (called kasha, if they're toasted) or ground into buckwheat flour. It's gluten-free and high in fiber. Compared to rice, wheat, and corn, buckwheat has more protein and is lower on the glycemic scale, so your blood sugar levels don't go on a wild ride.

⅓ cup whole, raw buckwheat groats

Fine sea salt

2 fresh apricots, quartered

2 tablespoons slivered almonds

1 tablespoon chia seeds

1 tablespoon honey

1 In a small pot, combine the buckwheat, ⅔ cup water, and a pinch of salt and bring to a boil. Reduce the heat to a simmer, cover, and cook until the groats are tender, about 12 minutes. Turn off the heat.

2 Add the apricots, almonds, chia seeds, and honey. Fold everything together, cover, and let sit until the apricots soften, 3 to 5 minutes.

Clockwise from bottom: old-fashioned rolled oats, steel-cut oats, and whole buckwheat groats.

SPINACH SCRAMBLED EGGS SERVES 1

This is my year-round, easy, too-tired-to-think-but-I'm-in-a-rush-and-gotta-eat-something breakfast. Even when we're down to the last dregs of food before a grocery trip, we always have garlic, frozen spinach, and eggs around. It's not the fastest breakfast in the world by America's current standards (of grabbing a donut or dumping milk over cereal), but it's pretty damn fast and about ten times as healthy. In about 5 minutes, you've got something hot, delicious, and good for you. ∎

1 tablespoon extra virgin olive oil

1 garlic clove, thinly sliced

2 extra-large eggs

Fine sea salt and freshly ground black pepper

¾ cup frozen chopped spinach

Any cheese you like, for serving (optional)

1 In a cold 10-inch skillet, combine the olive oil and garlic, then turn the heat to medium-high. Cook the garlic just long enough to heat through, 1 to 1½ minutes. Whisk the eggs in a bowl and season with salt and pepper.

2 When the garlic starts to sizzle, add the frozen spinach. Toss with the oil and garlic until the spinach is fully coated. Cover the pan for 30 seconds to thaw the spinach, then season with salt and pepper.

3 Pour the eggs over the spinach and cook for about 15 seconds. Stir by moving a silicone spatula across the bottom of the pan, flipping the eggs as they cook. Continue moving and flipping until the eggs are soft without any runny parts, about 2 minutes (longer if you like firmer, drier eggs).

4 Transfer to a plate and while the eggs are steaming, grate or crumble any cheese you like over the eggs.

EGGS

In the world of dietary myths, there may be none bigger than the one about eggs, skyrocketing the cholesterol of anyone who eats the occasional omelet. Maybe you've avoided them, or chosen to eat only egg whites or egg substitutes. But there is nothing inherently bad about eggs: They're actually one of the most perfect foods. Current research suggests there is little to no connection between dietary cholesterol and higher levels of blood cholesterol in humans.

I'm an advocate of eating whole eggs: The yolk houses half the protein and almost all of the vitamin A, good fat, and iron and the flavor. Eggs are also one of the few foods that offer vitamin D, an essential vitamin that most people are deficient in. The most important factor to consider when buying eggs is the source, ideally from pasture-raised chickens, not factory farms (see page 200 for the difference). I buy local, pasture-raised eggs or organic eggs whenever possible since those chickens were able to roam freely without the need for antibiotics because they're eating a natural diet. The deep, dark yellow of the yolks and stiff jelly-like whites carry significantly more flavor and nutritional benefits than regular eggs.

HARD-BOILED EGGS

I always keep hard-boiled eggs around. Talk about a quick, portable breakfast or snack— just peel and eat. I also like to chop them and toss them into green salads, where the cooked yolks add a silky richness. Hard-boiled eggs are easy to overcook. The telltale sign is that gross, greenish-gray ring around the yolk: While the taste isn't affected, the texture is shot to hell. Avoid that by bringing the eggs to a boil gently and using your kitchen timer. With the method here, I get perfect hard-boiled eggs every time. ■

1 Put the eggs in a single layer in a pot and fill it with cold water, covering the eggs by an inch or so. Bring the water to a boil over medium-high heat.

2 When the water starts boiling, take the pot off the heat, cover, and let it sit for 10 minutes.

3 Cool down the eggs. You can use a spoon to get them out of the pot and into a bowl with ice water, or pour the hot water out of the pot and fill with cold water.

BRAISED GREENS WITH SUNNY SIDE-UP EGGS SERVES 1

This is another variation on one of my favorite breakfasts of greens and eggs. It's a one-pan deal and can be ready in 5 minutes if you make the greens ahead of time in a big batch. Just reheat the greens in the pan, then pick up with step 3 in the recipe. I usually have cooked Tuscan kale on hand (aka lacinato kale or dinosaur kale), but any variety of sturdy greens works well here, including curly kale, Swiss chard, mustard greens, and collard greens. I don't recommend using fresh spinach—its high water content leads to watery eggs. ■

1 tablespoon plus 1 teaspoon extra virgin olive oil

½ small white onion, thinly sliced

1 small garlic clove, thinly sliced

Fine sea salt and freshly ground black pepper

2 cups packed Tuscan kale leaves, stems and center ribs removed

2 extra-large eggs

1 In a 10-inch skillet, heat 1 tablespoon of the oil over medium-high heat. Add the onion, garlic, and a pinch of salt. Cook until the onions are soft and translucent, about 5 minutes.

2 Add the greens and another pinch of salt. Stir well to coat the greens with the oil and onions. Reduce the heat to medium, cover the pan, and cook for 8 minutes, stirring every couple of minutes, until the kale is very tender. If you notice the greens start to look dry, add a teaspoon of water.

3 Reduce the heat to low and make a well in the center of the pan by pushing the greens to the edges. Add the remaining 1 teaspoon oil to the well and crack the eggs over it. Season with salt and pepper, cover the pan, and cook until the whites of the eggs are set, about 3 minutes.

MONTECASTELLI EGGS SERVES 4

This dish is inspired by an incredibly memorable moment from Montecastelli, a 1,000-year-old restored villa in Tuscany where I lead a weeklong cooking class every July. The villa is a food paradise with sprawling vegetable and herb gardens, a pasture of pigs and chickens, and an olive grove of 3,000 trees. The owner, Jens Schmidt, built a small bottling plant so he's able to harvest, press, and bottle olive oil in less than 48 hours. It's the freshest, most amazing olive oil, with the nice grassiness and intense peppery heat that Tuscan oils are famous for. The first time I visited, Jens made me a dish that showcased his oil: He sautéed fresh kale, kohlrabi, and leeks, cracked an egg over them, bathed it all in the olive oil, and baked it. It was a simple, beautiful, insanely rich dish that spoke to everything Montecastelli has to offer. Now I make it as a weekend breakfast or when we have friends over for brunch. I like using kale here because it doesn't release liquid the way spinach and Swiss chard do. ■

Don't let kohlrabi's alien-looking exterior put you off—it tastes like a mild, sweet turnip and adds a light crunch to this otherwise soft, silky egg dish.

¾ cup plus 2 tablespoons extra virgin olive oil

1 garlic clove, thinly sliced

2 small leeks, white and pale green parts only, thinly sliced, washed

1 bunch red Russian kale, stems and center ribs removed, leaves chopped (about 2 packed cups)

1 large kohlrabi bulb, peeled, halved, and thinly sliced

Fine sea salt and freshly ground black pepper

4 extra-large eggs

1 Preheat the oven to 300°F.

2 In a cold large skillet, combine 2 tablespoons of the oil, the garlic, and leeks, then turn the heat to high. Cook for 2 minutes, stirring to coat the garlic and leeks in oil, then reduce the heat to medium. Continue cooking for another 3 minutes to soften the leeks. Stir in the kale, kohlrabi, a pinch of salt and several grinds of pepper. Cover the pan and cook for 5 minutes, stirring occasionally. (You want the kale and kohlrabi to cook down, but they don't have to be completely soft. A little texture is good here.)

3 Divide the vegetables evenly among four (12-ounce) ramekins. Top each pile of vegetables with 2 tablespoons olive oil. Crack an egg into each ramekin and top each egg with 1 tablespoon olive oil and a pinch of salt and pepper.

4 Set the ramekins in a large, straight-sided pan (a roasting pan or casserole dish will work fine) and fill the pan with water until it's halfway up the sides of the ramekins. Cover the pan loosely with foil and bake for 35 minutes, or until the whites are set and the yolks are warm and runny. Serve the ramekins at the table.

APPLE WALNUT SPICE MUFFINS MAKES 12 MUFFINS

To my daughter Stella, these muffins are worthy of the same excitement as a set of new colored pencils or anything covered in glitter. (That's high praise from a seven-year-old girl.) All she cares about is that they're finger food and shaped like a cupcake. I like that these muffins are tender and moist with a light sweetness that sneaks through the deeper flavor of the warm spices. Also, the varying texture you get from the walnuts and the combination of grated apple and chopped apple keep the muffin interesting long after the first few bites. ∎

I use rye and oat flours because they're lower on the glycemic index than white flour, and they add a heartiness that I'm looking for in the morning, especially in the fall and winter when we have these as grab 'n' go breakfasts. Each one gets a smear of almond butter and we're out the door.

All nuts have good fat, protein, and fiber, but walnuts are considered the most heart-healthy because they have more omega-3 fatty acids and a higher level of antioxidants than other commonly eaten nuts. It only takes a handful a day to get the benefits, so have a few raw ones along with your muffin.

Unsalted butter, for greasing the muffin tin

1 cup rye flour

1 cup oat flour

⅓ cup ground flaxseed

1 tablespoon ground cinnamon

1 teaspoon ground ginger

½ teaspoon freshly grated nutmeg

¼ teaspoon ground cloves

1 teaspoon baking soda

Pinch of fine sea salt

3 medium Gala apples

1 extra-large egg, beaten

½ cup full-fat plain Greek yogurt

½ cup chopped walnuts plus 12 walnut halves

¼ cup extra virgin olive oil

1 tablespoon unsulfured blackstrap molasses

½ cup honey

1 Preheat the oven to 325°F. Butter a standard 12-cup muffin tin.

2 In a large bowl, mix the flours, flaxseed, cinnamon, ginger, nutmeg, cloves, baking soda, and salt until they're well combined.

3 Chop one of the apples into a small dice. Grate the remaining 2 apples on a box grater into a bowl. Add the diced apples, egg, yogurt, chopped walnuts, olive oil, molasses, and honey and whisk together.

4 Add the wet ingredients to the flour mixture and stir until they're just combined. Divide the batter evenly among the muffin cups; the filling should be almost level with the top of the tin. Lightly press a walnut half into the middle of each muffin.

5 Bake until the edges are golden brown and a toothpick inserted near the walnut comes out clean, 28 to 30 minutes. Let the muffins cool in the pan for 5 minutes, then take them out to finish cooling on a wire rack.

CORN AND BLUEBERRY MUFFINS MAKES 12 MUFFINS

In the summer when the market is bursting with blueberries, set aside some of your bounty to make these muffins. They have a distinctive, but not overwhelming, corn flavor that plays well with sweet blueberries and the pep of lemon zest. There's no exact science behind the combination of flours here—we tend to keep a wide variety on hand and I toy around with different combinations. I found that the thicker, high-fiber flours like coconut and whole wheat work best with the light, smooth texture of corn flour (not to be confused with cornmeal or cornstarch). ■

Fresh blueberries are the preferred way to go with this, but frozen berries will work.

Unsalted butter, for greasing the muffin tin

1 cup corn flour

¼ cup coconut flour

¾ cup whole wheat flour

Grated zest of 1 lemon

2 cups blueberries

1 teaspoon baking powder

½ teaspoon baking soda

Pinch of fine sea salt

2 extra-large eggs

1¼ cups buttermilk

½ teaspoon pure vanilla extract

¼ cup virgin coconut oil

½ cup coconut palm sugar

1 Preheat the oven to 325°F. Butter a standard 12-cup muffin tin.

2 In a large bowl, combine the flours, lemon zest, blueberries, baking powder, baking soda, and salt.

3 In a separate bowl, whisk together the eggs, buttermilk, vanilla, coconut oil, and coconut sugar. Add the wet ingredients to the dry mixture, and stir until they're just combined. Divide the batter evenly among the muffin cups.

4 Bake, until the edges are light brown and a toothpick inserted in the center of a muffin comes out clean, for 28 to 30 minutes. Let the muffins cool in the pan for 5 minutes, then take them out to finish cooling on a wire rack.

AMANDA'S BREAD MAKES 1 LOAF

I'm not fanatical about avoiding gluten, but we tend to keep it to a minimum at home because my wife finds she feels better without it. The frozen, gluten-free bricks at the store are a sorry excuse for bread, so through some trial and error (inevitable when baking without wheat flour), we came up with a simple recipe that yields a moist, tender loaf. It's dense, but not heavy, and the mild flavor of almonds gives the bread versatility for any sweet or savory toppings you want to throw on it. I love it toasted with blueberry jam. ∎

The batter will seem very wet. Resist the temptation to give it more flour—that will put your bread in dry, crumbly territory.

Many people see the gluten-free label on foods and assume this means they're inherently healthy, but gluten-free products are often heavily processed and loaded with added starches (many in the form of simple carbs), sugars, and chemical additives. Unless you have celiac disease or gluten sensitivity, you're better off sticking with minimally processed whole-grain foods. I've found that by eating mostly whole, real foods, I naturally eat less gluten—the only place I get it is via whole grains and flours like farro, rye, and spelt.

1½ cups almond flour

2 tablespoons coconut flour

¼ cup ground flaxseed

Pinch of fine sea salt

1½ teaspoons baking soda

5 large eggs, at room temperature

¼ cup extra virgin olive oil, plus more for the pan

1 tablespoon chestnut honey (or any dark-hued honey)

1 tablespoon apple cider vinegar

1 Preheat the oven to 350°F. Lightly coat a 9 × 5-inch nonstick loaf pan with olive oil.

2 In a food processor, combine the flours, ground flaxseed, salt, and baking soda. Pulse until the ingredients come together. Add the eggs, olive oil, honey, and vinegar and pulse until the wet ingredients are thoroughly combined with the dry.

3 Scrape the batter into the pan and bake until a toothpick inserted into the center of the loaf comes out clean, 35 to 40 minutes. Let it cool in the pan.

SOFT-BOILED EGG AND WHITE ANCHOVY BREAKFAST SANDWICHES MAKES 2 SANDWICHES

Like any good New Yorker, I have a soft spot for the classic bacon-egg-and-cheese-on-a-roll breakfast sandwich. It's the perfect little handheld meal when you want something fast and filling. The processed cheese, conventional bacon, and white bread they use at the corner deli aren't a regular part of my program anymore, so breakfast sandwiches are more of a homemade thing for me now. A runny, soft-cooked egg smashed on toast and topped with salty, tart white anchovies tastes incredible and feels pretty extravagant, although it's just a handful of ingredients—exactly what a breakfast sandwich should be.

I'm always on the lookout for whole-grain bread options, and my latest find is Nordic Breads' Finnish Ruis—rye flatbreads made from 100 percent whole-grain rye and a sourdough starter. They're sold in perfect sandwich-size rounds that we keep in the freezer and pop in the toaster. Chickpea Crepes (page 126) also work well for wrapping up a fast breakfast; so does Amanda's Bread (page 47) for lightweight fillings such as almond butter and jam. ∎

2 large eggs

1 Finnish Ruis bread, 1 English muffin, or 2 slices regular bread

2 tablespoons chopped fresh parsley

6 white anchovy fillets

Fine sea salt and freshly ground black pepper

1 Fill a pot about halfway with water and bring it to a boil over high heat. Use a large spoon to lower the eggs in their shells into the water one at a time. Reduce the heat to medium-high and cook the eggs for 6 to 7 minutes—6 minutes for a runnier yolk and 7 minutes for a tighter, thicker yolk. While the eggs are cooking, toast the bread.

2 When the eggs are cooked, remove them from the heat immediately and gently run cold tap water over them until they're cool enough to be handled. Carefully crack the eggs with a light tap and peel them like hard-boiled eggs.

3 Use a fork to mash 1 egg on each piece of toasted bread. Top each egg with a sprinkle of parsley and 3 anchovy fillets, and season with salt and pepper.

More of my favorite breakfast sandwich combinations to try:

- Sunny-side up egg, slice of cheddar, slice of tomato, flaky sea salt
- Crushed hard-boiled egg with olive oil and a spoonful of leftover cooked greens
- Sliced Cured Salmon (page 177) with red onion and capers
- Salt-cured anchovies and butter
- Sliced avocado, balsamic vinegar, flaky sea salt
- Almond butter and apple or pear slices
- Crunchy peanut butter with fork-smashed berries
- Sliced bananas and raw honey
- Grass-fed butter and any type of jam
- Leftover pieces of Herb-Roasted Spatchcock Chicken (page 216) with a smear of avocado and slice of tomato

BLUEBERRY AND BUCKWHEAT
BUTTERMILK PANCAKES MAKES 10 TO 12 PANCAKES

Sunday mornings are all about pancakes in my house. We don't stray from blueberry often, but we experiment with all kinds of flour combinations. This mix of whole wheat, corn, and buckwheat flours delivers exactly what I want in a pancake: hearty, slightly nutty flavor and a light, airy texture. With more fiber from whole grains, these are significantly better for you and more satisfying than the pathetically thin, processed white flour, nutritionally void pancakes. The batter should be thick and on the lumpy side: smooth batter makes tough pancakes. ∎

Cornmeal is not the same thing as corn flour and will give your pancakes a gritty texture along the lines of cornbread.

1 cup whole wheat flour
½ cup buckwheat flour
½ cup corn flour
1 teaspoon baking soda
1 teaspoon baking powder
½ teaspoon fine sea salt
2 cups buttermilk
¼ cup whole milk
1 extra-large egg
¼ cup virgin coconut oil
Unsalted butter, for the pan
¾ cup frozen wild blueberries, thawed
Maple syrup, for serving

1 In a large bowl, stir together the flours, baking soda, baking powder, and salt. In a separate bowl, whisk together the buttermilk, whole milk, and egg. Then whisk in the coconut oil. Add the wet ingredients to the dry and mix until just combined. (The batter will be very thick, so don't worry about small lumps.)

2 Heat a large skillet or griddle over high heat and add a small pat of butter. When the butter melts and goes brown, pour in ⅓ cup of the pancake batter. Sprinkle 1 tablespoon frozen blueberries on top and press them into the batter. Cook until bubbles form on the surface and the edges harden, 1 to 2 minutes. Flip and cook until the bottom is golden, about 1½ minutes. Transfer the pancake to a plate and cover it to keep warm.

3 Repeat with the remaining batter, adding more butter to the pan when needed. Serve the pancakes warm with maple syrup.

SALADS

THERE'S NO BETTER VEHICLE THAN a salad for packing a range of flavors, textures, proteins, good fats, and a variety of vegetables into one meal. So, why do so many people think salads are a bore, or a side dish to be eaten out of obligation? For starters, the diet food connotation is a turnoff. It brings up images of pathetic "garden salads," wilted, brownish iceberg lettuce garnished with a slab of under-ripe tomato and limp cucumber slices. When you start to rethink what a salad can be, things get exciting—you start to crave them.

To make salads appealing in the long run, you have to venture beyond the standard bowl of lettuce leaves. A salad can be just about any combination of vegetables, meat, fish, beans, or grains bound together by acidity (citrus, vinegar, pickling liquid) and good fat (usually extra virgin olive oil, occasionally bacon fat or duck fat). Give the tried-and-true foundation of leafy greens a few good sidekicks, and you get a wider variety of nutrients that also keep your hunger pangs quiet longer. I prefer hardy greens like Tuscan kale, escarole, dandelion greens, and spinach as a base because they stand up to dressing. Besides having a ho-hum nutritional profile, iceberg and romaine lettuce have high water content and often lead to the tragedy that is soggy salads.

Inevitably, you'll need a break from leafy greens. As I eat salads a lot more frequently now, this happens to me too. That's when I break out my simple mandoline slicer and build a salad with paper-thin coins and ribbons of firm raw vegetables. One of my favorites is the bright, massively crunchy Shaved Fennel, Celery, Red Onion, and Parsley Salad (page 74). This method works equally well with raw asparagus, beets, turnips, onions, carrots, kohlrabi, radishes, artichokes, zucchini, cucumbers, and cauliflower.

Another way to keep things interesting is to play with temperature. The Warm Vegetable Salad (page 73) shows the beauty of one of my simple go-to techniques for ramping up flavor in salads: dressing things while they're hot. Vegetables' pores open up as you cook them, allowing them to take on more flavor by drinking in olive oil, vinegar, and salt. Temperature contrast keeps me coming back to salads: the juicy pop of orange segments in the Roasted Beet Salad (page 78) and the hot caramelized fennel in the Spinach Salad with Roasted Fennel (page 69) give these otherwise simple dishes more character and depth of flavor. Every forkful is a different experience.

Without the right combination of oil and vinegar and proper seasoning to punctuate the flavors, even a salad of the freshest seasonal ingredients and rock-solid combination of textures and temperatures will fall flat. The perky, well-balanced vinaigrettes here will do your salad justice: Each one is versatile enough to become your house dressing. I'm partial to simply dressing a salad in the bowl it's served in. I give it a glug of whatever vinegar I'm in the mood for (usually red wine vinegar), a drizzle of extra virgin olive oil, and a sprinkling of salt and pepper, and hand-toss it all. I can't tell you how many people I've made salads for over the years commented, "Wow, this is so delicious! How did you make the vinaigrette?" Just vinegar, salt, pepper, and oil—no whisking necessary. If you use this approach, always add the vinegar and salt before the oil. Otherwise, the oil coats everything and acts as a barrier, preventing the salt from dissolving and the vinegar from mingling with the other flavors.

A word on processed salad dressings: don't. Most of them are dull glop filled with preservatives, high-fructose corn syrup, salt, and bad fat from canola or soybean oil. There's no way to justify buying them when it's so easy (and more affordable) to shake up a few quality ingredients in a jar or use my on-the-fly method of dressing.

VINAIGRETTES

A good vinaigrette seasons, adds moisture, brightens flavors, and brings all the elements of a salad in tune with each other.

The ratio of oil to acid is the main consideration. I don't know what vinaigrette overlord came up with the standard ratio of 3:1, but I find it to be complete nonsense. The taste for acidity (from things like vinegar and citrus) is like the taste for salt—there's no formula, it's what tastes right to you. So, the ratio is really a personal preference. Also, acidity levels vary widely among different types of vinegar. Some sherry vinegars are intensely acidic, while some mild balsamic vinegars out there barely have any acidity. A successful ratio of oil to acid also depends on the ingredients in the salad you're dressing. For example, in a salad with starches like potatoes or beans, you will likely want a higher proportion of vinegar to brighten their heavier flavor. I like salads with a bite of acid from lots of lemon juice and vinegar. If you find any of the vinaigrettes in this section to be too tart, feel free to add more oil—follow your taste buds, not a formula.

I'm all for as little cleanup as possible, so I make salad dressings in leftover glass jars. That way, I can just screw the lid on and shake it up, rather than pull out a bowl and whisk. Vinaigrettes can be stored in the refrigerator for about 5 days, so I recommend making a batch or two each week. If the olive oil hardens in the fridge, bring it to room temperature by running some warm water over the outside of the jar, and give it a few good shakes before using.

THE POWER OF ALKALINE FOODS

(aka What I Learned from My Big Toe)

"Gout? Seriously?" I was completely thrown by my doctor's diagnosis. I'd heard gout ridiculed as the "disease of kings," something only gluttonous fat dudes (like Henry VIII) got. Sure, I had recurring foot pain, mostly in my heels and big toe, but I chalked it up to long hours at the restaurant. And I knew my diet was a far cry from the picture of health, but . . . gout?! It's another lesson on the list of things I've learned the hard way.

Gout is an inflammatory condition caused by a crazy-high level of uric acid in the body. The excess uric acid forms crystals that collect in joints and cause painful swelling. Burgers and deli meats, as well as yeast-filled bread and beer, are high in a compound called purine, and purine breaks down into uric acid in the body. It's normal to have a supply of uric acid, but when there's too much, your kidneys can't eliminate it fast enough, and it starts building up in places it shouldn't. The more of those purine-rich foods I ate, the more uric acid accumulated in my joints, and the more my big toe hurt. To throw it in reverse, I had to start eating foods that would reduce my inflammation.

Digging into what this meant for my day-to-day eating habits, I came across the theory of the alkaline diet. The theory is that loading up on alkaline-forming foods and limiting acid-forming foods helps your body reduce inflammation by maintaining the ideal pH balance for peak health. Why more alkaline foods? The typical American diet, with all its meat, refined sugar, caffeine, and processed foods, dumps a steady stream of acid into your blood, so you need more foods that are alkaline, the opposite of acidic, to balance things out. Otherwise, your overly acidic body may resort to maintaining pH balance by pilfering its own store of minerals, making you more vulnerable to chronic inflammation and disease.

Taking control of my inflammation-induced gout led me to curb my habit of beer and meat-filled deli sandwiches, and to fill in those holes with the alkaline superstars, namely green vegetables like kale, spinach, lettuces, and dandelion greens, which I use in the salads here. Wheatgrass is the king of alkaline foods, but the alkaline-friendly foods in regular rotation in my kitchen are tomatoes, squash, avocado, root veggies, most fruit—especially citrus—seeds, and some nuts and legumes. Though meat and fish can be acidic, a few times a week I'll have grass-fed beef and wild salmon, which are high in anti-inflammatory omega-3 fatty acids (see page 174).

The beauty of the alkaline approach is that it's about balance, so eating a moderate amount of unrefined acidic foods is still okay. Most of the recommendations you'll find suggest that at least 60 percent of your foods be alkaline-forming and no more than 40 percent be acid-forming. But some foods don't have to taste acidic to lead to an acid party in your body. For example, a sugar-laden pastry is acid-forming, while acidic tasting foods like lemons and vinegar are alkaline-forming. And there are a few foods that fit into an alkaline diet, but don't work for gout-sufferers because they're

high in purines (lentils, for example). This may sound tricky, but trust me, it's not. Unless you have a throbbing big toe right now, focus on cutting back on refined sugar, meat, and packaged foods, and make up for them with more greens and fruit, especially citrus.

My experience with inflammation and gout made me a believer in the alkaline approach. I felt noticeable relief within four months of changing my diet, and now I'm gout-free. While I don't think there's one healthy diet theory that's a home run for everyone, it's hard to poke holes in a style of eating that emphasizes fresh, plant-based, unprocessed food. Even if you don't buy into the pH aspect, eating more alkaline foods will do you right.

HONEY-CIDER VINAIGRETTE MAKES ABOUT 1⅓ CUPS

Another workhorse vinaigrette, this one lends itself to sturdier lettuces like romaine, kale, red oak, and escarole that can hold up to the higher proportion of vinegar used here. ■

¼ cup plus 2 tablespoons apple cider vinegar

Several pinches of fine sea salt

3 tablespoons honey

¾ cup extra virgin olive oil

Add all the ingredients to a screw-top jar. Screw the lid on tightly and shake well to combine.

MAPLE SYRUP VINAIGRETTE MAKES ABOUT 1 CUP

Maple syrup brings a richness to the vinaigrette while mellowing out the sharper flavors of fresh ginger and vinegar. This plays well with wintry greens like red oak leaf lettuce, frisée, or watercress mixed with thinly sliced apple or pear. It's also a great pairing for hearty fall vegetables like sweet potatoes, carrots, turnips, and those in the Maple and Spice–Roasted Autumn Squash (page 100). ■

3 tablespoons apple cider vinegar

Pinch of fine sea salt

3 tablespoons maple syrup

1½ teaspoons grated fresh ginger

⅔ cup extra virgin olive oil

Add all the ingredients to a screw-top jar. Screw the lid on tightly and shake well to combine.

SOY-GINGER VINAIGRETTE MAKES ABOUT 1 CUP

When I need a change of pace from standard vinaigrettes, the big, bold Asian flavors of soy, ginger, and sesame call to me. The saltiness of soy sauce combined with the pungent, bright heat from the ginger acts like a spark plug, adding a kick to anything you dress with this. It's a great match for sturdy greens such as bok choy (see page 189, Steamed Black Bass with Bok Choy), escarole, romaine, and spinach, and can be used as a marinade for chicken, pork, or shrimp. I also like to add a glug to a hot bowl of sweet brown rice. ∎

2 tablespoons rice vinegar (lime juice works nicely too)

2 tablespoons fresh lemon juice

2 teaspoons grated fresh ginger

¼ cup soy sauce

2 teaspoons toasted sesame oil

½ cup extra virgin olive oil

Add all the ingredients to a screw-top jar. Screw the lid on tightly and shake well to combine.

HONEY-TANGERINE DRESSING MAKES ABOUT 1 CUP

Tangerine juice replaces vinegar in this great sweet-tart dressing. The juice from tangerines and other citrus fruits is smoother and less acidic than most vinegars, so I use an equal proportion of juice to oil. To keep this light and bright, use a fruity or floral honey here. It pairs nicely with softer, buttery lettuces like Bibb, red leaf, and green leaf varieties. ∎

½ cup fresh tangerine juice

Pinch of fine sea salt

1 tablespoon honey

½ cup extra virgin olive oil

Add all the ingredients to a screw-top jar. Screw the lid on tightly and shake well to combine.

FERMENTED CARROT AND GINGER VINAIGRETTE MAKES ABOUT 1 CUP

Fermented carrots and ginger pull double duty here, adding a lively tartness to the vinaigrette, along with a high level of digestion-friendly natural probiotics (see page 95 for more on these). If you don't have a batch of fermented carrots and ginger on hand, use 1 cup shredded regular carrots and 1 tablespoon grated fresh ginger. ∎

¾ cup Lacto-Fermented Carrots and Ginger (page 94)

1 tablespoon miso paste

1 tablespoon toasted sesame oil

2 tablespoons brown rice vinegar

1 tablespoon soy sauce or tamari

½ cup extra virgin olive oil

In a blender, combine the carrots and ginger, miso, sesame oil, vinegar, and soy sauce. While pureeing, add the olive oil in a steady stream until the vinaigrette is smooth.

TUSCAN KALE SALAD WITH WHITE BEANS AND TUNA SERVES 4

I was actually eating kale long before it was anointed the "it" vegetable, mostly in the Italian soups and stews I grew up on. But I added raw Tuscan kale to the classic combination of cannellini beans, tuna, and red onions. I never thought a salad could approach comfort food status, but this one is so satisfying that I crave it regularly. I prefer the dark, bumpy leaves of Tuscan kale to curly leaf kale for salads because they have a more delicate flavor and tender texture. ∎

1 (6-ounce) can olive oil–packed tuna, drained

1 bunch Tuscan kale, stems and center ribs removed, leaves chopped into bite-size pieces (about 4 cups)

2 cups cooked cannellini beans (page 113) or 1 (15-ounce) can cannellini beans, rinced and drained

½ medium red onion, thinly sliced

2 tablespoons red wine vinegar

¼ cup extra virgin olive oil

Fine sea salt and freshly ground black pepper

In a large bowl, flake the tuna into bite-size pieces with a fork. Add the kale, beans, onion, vinegar, and oil and season with salt and pepper to taste. Toss gently to combine.

It's worth splurging for the imported Italian or Spanish tuna packed in extra virgin olive oil. They're infinitely more flavorful then regular tuna packed in water. Homemade beans' firmer texture is ideal in this salad, but you can substitute canned beans; just rinse and drain them well.

LEMON VINAIGRETTE WITH GARLIC AND ANCHOVY MAKES ABOUT 1 CUP

Acidity from fresh lemon, a good fat like olive oil, some garlic, and the salty flavor of anchovies add up to a dressing that brightens all kinds of dishes. Toss it with leafy greens or shaved vegetable salads, drizzle over steamed pieces of fish, or pour a tablespoon over Herb-Roasted Spatchcock Chicken (page 216) or Rosemary-Lemon Minute Steak (page 225). ■

Juice of 1 lemon

1 garlic clove, peeled

2 olive oil–packed anchovy fillets

Fine sea salt and freshly ground black pepper

¾ cup extra virgin olive oil

1 Squeeze the lemon juice into a screw-top glass jar. Cut the garlic clove in half across its equator; smash each half with the flat side of a large knife. Mince the garlic and anchovies together, add a pinch of salt, and mash into a smooth paste with a knife. Add it to the jar.

2 Add the olive oil and a pinch of salt and pepper. Screw the lid on the jar and shake to combine. Taste and add more lemon juice or seasoning, if needed.

DANDELION SALAD WITH HARD-BOILED EGGS SERVES 4 TO 6

This is one of my favorite salads. It also happens to be one of the easiest, quickest salads to throw together. A few bunches of nicely bitter dandelion greens are simply dressed with red wine vinegar, olive oil, and hard-boiled eggs. As you combine everything, the vinegar breaks down some of the egg, creating a thin, rich coating that mutes the bitterness of the greens. When I was growing up, my mom cooked dandelion greens a lot, saying fresh dandelions clean your blood. She knows her stuff—that naturally bitter flavor is actually a sign of dandelion's detox power. So if you eat a bunch of heavy, fatty, or processed foods, do your liver a favor and dig in on this salad for some cleansing action. ■

Many of the nutrients in leafy green vegetables are fat-soluble, which means they need to be eaten with some fat so that your body can adequately absorb the nutrients. Eggs and olive oil provide the fat in this salad, but nuts, avocado, and cheese do the job too.

2 bunches dandelion greens, thick stems removed, cut into 2-inch pieces (about 6 cups)

4 Hard-Boiled Eggs (page 40), chopped

½ medium red onion, thinly sliced

2 tablespoons red wine vinegar

¼ cup extra virgin olive oil

Fine sea salt and freshly ground black pepper

Crumbled croutons or toasted breadcrumbs (optional)

Put all the ingredients (except the croutons, if using) in a large salad bowl and really get in there with your hands to thoroughly mix everything so the egg yolks break down and coat the greens. Sprinkle with croutons or toasted breadcrumbs, if you like.

TOMATO AND PEACH SALAD SERVES 4 TO 6

This refreshing salad is one to make in the summer, when the farmers' markets are blowing up with big, fat, juicy tomatoes, and peaches are at their height of sweetness. The two are perfect together, with the peaches balancing the acidity of the tomatoes. Thai basil is a bit spicier than regular sweet basil, and the purple tinge on the leaves adds more color to the mix. No biggie if you can't find it—sweet basil is great here too. My farmers' market occasionally carries small yellow cucumbers that I'll snatch up for this, along with a couple of colors of heirloom tomatoes. Don't resist the urge to add cheese, if that sounds good to you. Use a dry, crumbly goat cheese, feta, or ricotta salata. ∎

This salad doesn't stick around long, so if it's been a day and you still have some left, dump it in a blender and turn it into a gazpacho by adding a bit more vinegar and adjusting the salt to taste.

2 large ripe tomatoes, cut into large chunks

2 peaches, cut into wedges

1 small cucumber, thinly sliced

¼ cup Thai basil leaves

1 tablespoon balsamic vinegar

Fine sea salt

2 tablespoons extra virgin olive oil

1 On a platter or in a large, shallow serving bowl, combine the tomatoes, peaches, and cucumber. Tear the basil leaves and scatter them over the top.

2 Drizzle the vinegar over the salad, add salt to taste, and pour on the olive oil. Toss gently.

ESCAROLE SALAD WITH PEAR AND PECORINO SERVES 4 TO 6

We serve this classic winter salad at Hearth, but I often make it at home too because it comes together fast. Escarole is a sturdy, leafy lettuce that's high in fiber and beta carotene, which the body converts into vitamin A and vitamin K. Slightly bitter escarole and sweet pear are great mates, but what makes this hearty salad really sing is using the walnuts and cheese in two different forms. Finely grated cheese and ground walnuts coat the leaves, so their flavors permeate the whole salad. Shavings of cheese and chopped walnuts allow you to have bigger bursts of those flavors with some crunch. Don't be shy with the pepper here—it goes great with pecorino cheese. ■

1 head escarole, washed, cored, leaves torn into bite-size pieces

½ red onion, thinly sliced

1 Bosc pear, thinly sliced or shaved on a mandoline

½ cup toasted walnuts—¼ cup chopped and ¼ cup ground (do this with a coffee grinder)

¼ cup finely grated Pecorino Romano cheese, plus a small chunk for shaving on top

Honey-Cider Vinaigrette (page 58)

Fine sea salt and freshly ground black pepper

In a large bowl, combine the escarole, onion, pear, ground walnuts, and grated Pecorino. Add as much vinaigrette as you like, along with salt and a generous amount of pepper. Toss to combine. Scatter the chopped walnuts and Pecorino shavings over the top and serve.

MY POST-WORKOUT SALAD SERVES 1

On those crazy days when time and energy are in short supply, it's way too easy for me to fall into old food habits. I've found that the way to ace a good food day when I'm insanely busy is to plan ahead for leftovers that can be quickly combined in an energizing meal that's as exciting and crave-worthy as any trashy convenience food. This salad is all about using what you have on hand—leftovers plus a few pantry and refrigerator mainstays, chopped up and tossed with olive oil and vinegar.

I started making these salads after my daily workout and realized there's a simple formula that boosts my energy, fills me up without weighing me down, offers tons of nutrients, and has enough flavor and texture to keep it interesting. This salad is endlessly adaptable, so use this recipe as a template to give you inspiration. If you switch it up with different greens, proteins, vegetables, and dressings, you'll never get sick of this. Think about a couple simple things that you can keep on hand: White anchovies? Marinated artichokes? Oil-cured olives? Having your special something around will help pull you toward the salad. ∎

1 cup chopped dandelion greens

1 cup shredded or cubed cooked chicken

¼ cup cooked lentils

1 celery stalk, chopped

¼ red onion, sliced thinly

1 small garlic clove, grated

1 tablespoon pumpkin seeds

1 tablespoon sunflower seeds

¼ cup loosely packed flat-leaf parsley leaves, chopped

½ avocado, cut into chunks

1 tablespoon plus 1½ teaspoons red wine vinegar

1 tablespoon plus 1½ teaspoons extra virgin olive oil

Fine sea salt and freshly ground black pepper

In a salad bowl, combine the greens, chicken, lentils, celery, red onion, garlic, both seeds, parsley, avocado, vinegar, and olive oil. Add a couple pinches of salt and several grinds of pepper to taste. Toss well and dig in.

MY POST-WORKOUT SALAD BLUEPRINT

1 LEAFY GREEN—dandelion greens, spinach, Tuscan kale, Swiss chard, arugula

1 ANIMAL-SOURCED PROTEIN—chicken, salmon, sardines, hard-boiled egg, white or brown anchovies

1 TENDER BEAN OR GRAIN—lentils, cannellini beans, quinoa, millet

CRUNCHY VEGETABLES—celery, carrots, red bell peppers, cucumbers

1 TO 2 ONIONS—red onions, scallions, shallots, garlic

A HANDFUL OF HERBS—flat-leaf parsley, cilantro, basil

SLICES OF AVOCADO

1 OR 2 TYPES OF SEEDS OR NUTS—pumpkin seeds, sunflower seeds, sliced almonds, chopped walnuts

EXTRA VIRGIN OLIVE OIL AND VINEGAR OR CITRUS—red wine vinegar, apple cider vinegar, fresh lemon juice

FINE SEA SALT AND FRESHLY GROUND BLACK PEPPER

BIBB LETTUCE SALAD WITH BEE POLLEN SERVES 4

My wife, Amanda, brought home a jar of raw bee pollen after reading about its spectacular nutritional benefits, and it's been a staple in our fridge ever since. The soft, spongy yellow granules have a sweet and surprisingly complex, earthy flavor. I like it in oatmeal, smoothies, yogurt, and salads, and sprinkled over nut butter on toast. It's best as a finishing touch, since all the good stuff in bee pollen is destroyed by heat. Here, it plays well with the fruity tang of tangerines and gives a pop of texture to the salad. ■

A jar of bee pollen is a little pot of gold. It contains up to 35 percent protein and is high in B vitamins, so it's great for a natural boost of energy. A regular dose of fresh, local pollen gives some people relief from seasonal allergies because it helps build up resistance to the pollen floating around in the air. Ideally, you can buy local bee pollen from a vendor at your farmers' market, but you can also find it in most health food stores.

2 heads Bibb lettuce, separated into leaves

2 tangerines, divided into segments

2 tablespoons bee pollen

¼ cup Honey-Tangerine Dressing (page 59)

Fine sea salt and freshly ground black pepper

In a large salad bowl, combine the lettuce leaves, tangerine segments, bee pollen, and dressing. Season with salt and pepper to taste and gently toss to combine.

SPINACH SALAD WITH ROASTED FENNEL, OIL-CURED OLIVES, AND GRAPEFRUIT SERVES 4

I champion the use of fennel in any form, but it's hard to top roasted fennel. Roasting brings out its natural sweetness while concentrating its anise flavor. You can roast the fennel as long or as little as you like; it'll be just as good slightly roasted or cooked to brown crispiness. While I could easily eat roasted fennel like candy, tossing the warm wedges with raw spinach makes a compelling salad with a contrast of temperature and texture in every bite. The oil-cured black olives are a key element: They're really full-flavored and add a nice hit of salinity to the zing of grapefruit and the sweet, mellow licorice flavor of the roasted fennel. I like to cut the grapefruit into suprêmes, whole segments without the membrane. If you want to go a simpler route, cut the grapefruit in half across the equator, run your knife around the entire perimeter between the peel and the fruit, and then scoop out the grapefruit segments with a spoon or knife. ∎

1 large fennel bulb, halved lengthwise, and each half cut lengthwise into 8 to 10 thin wedges

Fine sea salt and freshly ground black pepper

3 tablespoons extra virgin olive oil

1 pink grapefruit

8 ounces baby spinach (about 6 loosely packed cups)

½ cup halved and pitted oil-cured black olives

1 Preheat the oven to 350°F. Line a baking sheet with foil.

2 Toss the fennel wedges with 1 tablespoon of the olive oil and salt and pepper to taste. Roast until they've softened and the edges are browned and crispy, about 30 minutes.

3 Meanwhile, use a Microplane or fine grater to grate the grapefruit zest into a bowl. Using a sharp knife, slice a thin piece of peel off the top and bottom ends of the grapefruit so it sits flat on the cutting board. Peel the grapefruit, following the curve of the fruit, to remove all the white pith and the membrane covering the fruit. Working over another bowl, cut in between the membranes to release the segments. Juice what's left of the grapefruit into the bowl with the segments.

4 In a large serving bowl, combine the spinach, olives, grapefruit segments (not the juice yet), and zest. As soon as the fennel is finished roasting, add it to the bowl along with about 2 tablespoons of the reserved grapefruit juice and the remaining 2 tablespoons olive oil. Add salt and pepper to taste and toss to combine.

SPINACH SALAD WITH ROASTED FENNEL, OIL-CURED OLIVES, AND GRAPEFRUIT (PAGE 69)

WARM VEGETABLE SALAD SERVES 4

This is a really tasty salad that you can adapt to whatever vegetables are in season. At Hearth, I make this in July when every variety of summer squash is happening, and I can find a boatload of varieties of pole beans, like green and yellow Romano beans (they look like large, flat green beans) and green, yellow, and purple string beans. If you want to go fancy with this, add more varieties and colors of zucchini, yellow squash, and string beans. You can also rely on a trio of standby vegetables, like green beans, onion, and potato or broccoli, cauliflower, and potato. Though you don't need much of it, the potato is key because it coats the vegetables, providing a subtle richness. Whatever combination of vegetables you go with, you want to cook them until they're soft, and drain them well before dressing them; otherwise, the salad is watered down and blah-tasting. ∎

When buying zucchini, the smaller and heavier, the better. The huge ones with spongy, soggy interiors soak up too much oil. Aim for zucchini that's no more than 1 inch in diameter.

½ cup thinly sliced red onion (about 1 small)

1 small garlic clove

2 tablespoons red wine vinegar

Fine sea salt and freshly ground black pepper

1 medium Yukon Gold potato, unpeeled and cut into 1-inch chunks

2 cups trimmed and halved string beans

1 medium green zucchini, halved lengthwise and cut crosswise into ½-inch slices (about 1 cup)

1 medium yellow squash, halved lengthwise and cut crosswise into ½-inch slices (about 1 cup)

3 tablespoons extra virgin olive oil

¼ cup chopped fresh basil

1 Add the onion to a large salad bowl and finely grate the garlic clove over it. Pour the red wine vinegar over the onion and garlic and season with a pinch of salt.

2 Bring a large pot of salted water to boil over high heat. Add the potato and cook for 6 minutes. Drop the string beans into the pot and cover. Cook for 3 minutes, then add the zucchini and squash. Cover and cook for 4 minutes, until all the vegetables are soft.

3 Drain the vegetables, letting them sit in the colander to cool for a couple of minutes. Fish out the potatoes and add them to the bowl with the onion and garlic. Lightly crush the potatoes with the tines of a fork, but don't mash them to oblivion. Transfer the drained vegetables to the bowl.

4 Add the olive oil and basil and season with salt and pepper. Toss to combine.

SHAVED FENNEL, CELERY, RED ONION, AND PARSLEY SALAD SERVES 4

Amidst all the heavy dishes of winter, I love to dig into this refreshing, crunchy, totally raw vegetable salad. If you've never tried fennel in its raw state, this salad is a great way to get into its crisp texture and mildly sweet, licorice-like flavor, matched up with celery, flashes of red onion, and the brightness of parsley. It's an easy one to throw together, but you need a mandoline (or infinite patience and good knife skills) in order to get the paper-thin slices of vegetables you want for this salad. My favorite tool for the job is a Benriner, a commonly available Japanese vegetable slicer. It's inexpensive and really broadens your repertoire by allowing you to make a quick salad out of any shaved sturdy vegetables and fruits you like. Anyone who dislikes the tediousness of chopping will become a big fan of the mandoline—and this salad. ■

If you can get your hands on one, shaving a fresh raw artichoke heart into this salad is a great idea.

If the Lemon Vinaigrette with Garlic and Anchovy isn't your thing, you can dress the salad with the juice of 1 lemon and 2 tablespoons extra virgin olive oil.

½ large fennel bulb, stalks discarded

½ red onion

4 celery heart stalks (the inner, pale green stalks)

¼ cup packed celery heart leaves

⅓ cup packed flat-leaf parsley leaves

3 tablespoons Lemon Vinaigrette with Garlic and Anchovy (page 61)

Fine sea salt and freshly ground black pepper

Parmigiano-Reggiano cheese shavings (optional)

1 Cut the fennel bulb in quarters lengthwise through the core. Slice each quarter thinly on a mandoline (to make about 1 packed cup). Halve the red onion half through the core and thinly slice. Thinly slice the celery heart stalks (for about ½ cup packed).

2 In a large bowl, combine the fennel, onion, celery slices and leaves, parsley, vinaigrette, and salt and pepper to taste. Toss to combine and adjust the seasoning, if needed. Top with a good dose of Parmesan shavings, if you like.

THAI-STYLE EGGPLANT SALAD SERVES 4

Eggplant's spongelike tendency is its greatest asset and its most common road to ruin. A little too much oil and it turns into a soggy mush. By dry-roasting it, eggplant comes out soft, but still maintains its meaty texture. Peeling away alternating strips of skin helps to hold the tender eggplant slices together after they're roasted and adds a flash of deep purple color to the salad, along with more fiber and antioxidants. Japanese eggplants are one of my favorite treasures at the summer greenmarket. Compared to globe and Italian varieties, Japanese eggplants have narrower, longer bodies with firm, sweet flesh and thinner skin. If you can't get them, substitute Italian eggplants. Both varieties take well to an Asian dressing that has a delicious intensity of salty and tart flavors combined with mild heat from a serrano pepper and fresh, green brightness from loads of cilantro, basil, and mint. ∎

Extra virgin olive oil, for the baking sheet

1½ pounds Japanese eggplant

2 tablespoons warm water

1 tablespoon coconut palm sugar

1 tablespoon fresh lime juice

2 tablespoons soy sauce

1 teaspoon fish sauce

1 bunch scallions, white and pale green parts only, thinly sliced

1 large garlic clove, finely grated

½ serrano chile, thinly sliced (leave it out or add more if you dig heat)

¼ cup loosely packed fresh mint leaves, torn

¼ cup loosely packed cilantro leaves, torn

¼ cup loosely packed fresh basil leaves, torn

1 Preheat the oven to 350°F. Line a baking sheet with foil and lightly coat it with olive oil.

2 Peel away alternating strips of skin lengthwise on each eggplant, leaving strips of unpeeled skin in between, so you get a racing stripe look. Cut the eggplant crosswise into ½-inch-thick rounds (1-inch cubes, if you're using regular eggplant) and arrange them in a single layer on the baking sheet. Roast until the eggplant slices are tender all the way to the center, about 30 minutes.

3 In a large bowl, whisk the water and coconut sugar together until the sugar dissolves. Add the lime juice, soy sauce, and fish sauce and whisk to combine. While it's still warm, add the roasted eggplant to the bowl of dressing. Drop in the scallions, garlic, serrano chile, mint, cilantro, and basil and toss to combine.

ROASTED BEET SALAD WITH BEET GREENS, ORANGES, AND PISTACHIOS SERVES 4

Instead of the standard approach of roasting beets whole and then peeling for a salad, I slice and roast them skin-on at a low temperature. A really cool thing happens texturally—they shrivel up a bit and the outsides become slightly dehydrated, giving a nice contrast to the still sweet and juicy inside. It's like biting into a beet-flavored gummy bear. Beet greens, the leafy tops that you usually cut off and discard, are blanched and chopped to form the base of the salad. They taste similar to Swiss chard and are a nutritional force in their own right. If you can, use a mix of different colored beets: combine red and golden, or see if your local market has the candy-striped or white varieties. This is a beauty of a dish, bright in flavor and color. ■

Since the beet skins aren't peeled off, be sure to scrub the outsides to clean them well.

5 medium beets with greens, trimmed and cut into ½-inch-thick slices, greens reserved

4 tablespoons extra virgin olive oil

Fine sea salt and freshly ground black pepper

2 oranges

¼ cup pistachios, chopped or cracked with bottom of a pot

1 Preheat the oven to 300°F. Line a baking sheet with foil.

2 In a bowl, toss the sliced beets with 2 tablespoons of the olive oil and season with salt and pepper. Arrange the beets in a single layer on the baking sheet. Bake for 30 minutes. Flip each slice and bake until the beets have shrunk in size a bit and the skins look dehydrated, another 30 minutes. (It's really up to your preference in texture, so give one a taste. If you want chewier beets, bake them a little longer.)

3 While the beets are baking, bring a pot of salted water to boil. Remove the center rib from the beet greens. Thoroughly wash the greens, then add them to the boiling water and blanch until tender, about 2 minutes. Drain into a colander and run cold water over them to stop the cooking. Squeeze the greens into a ball in your hand, wringing out as much liquid as possible. Put the ball on a cutting board and slice it like the grid of a tic-tac-toe board. Add the greens to a large bowl.

4 Working over the bowl of greens, grate the zest of one of the oranges. Juice half of the zested orange into the bowl. Using a sharp paring knife, cut all the peel, pith, and outer membranes from the second orange, and slice it crosswise into thin rounds.

5 While the beets are still warm, add them to the bowl of greens. Add the orange slices, the remaining 2 tablespoons olive oil, and the pistachios and toss to combine. Add salt and pepper to taste.

VEGETABLES

EVEN BACK IN MY DAYS OF EATING trashy foods, I've always been a vegetable fan. My mom and my aunt maintained elaborate gardens, so our meals revolved around whatever beautiful veggies were popping up at the moment. Meat might have been on the plate, but the protein didn't define the meal. Sometimes dinner was an egg dish full of vegetables, like my Japanese Sweet Potato and Cauliflower Frittata (page 108), or a vegetable-based pasta similar to Whole Wheat Rigatoni with Porcini Mushrooms and Baby Spinach (page 155). I fully support the growing trend toward vegetable-focused meals like these, so they get a lot of love in this book, especially here and in the salads and grains chapters. (There's a reason I put 'em way earlier than the meat and fish sections.)

Vegetables are the food kingdom's holy grail for a variety of vitamins, minerals, and antioxidants. You could give up carbs, meat, or dairy and still live a long, healthy life, but if you skip out on vegetables, all bets are off. The problem with the "eat your vegetables" message is that for too many people, it makes eating vegetables feel like a chore. We should focus on what's truly exciting about them— the mind-blowing diversity of colors, shapes, sizes, and textures, and the incredible potential for flavor. Consider the color spectrum alone and you'll see why I find more inspiration in vegetables than any other foods.

Vegetables also give you the ability to run the gamut of cooking techniques—braising, roasting, boiling, sautéing, dehydrating, pickling, fermenting, and everything in between. The opportunities you have are endless—and exciting to me both as a cook and as someone trying to eat mostly healthy foods every day. It's impossible to fall into a healthy eating rut if you're really taking advantage of the variety of vegetables and cooking methods available to you. Another point for vegetables is the volume you can consume—for those times when I can only be satisfied by a giant bowl of food (old habits die hard), vegetables allow me to chow down in a way that isn't disastrous to my body.

The idea of veggie-focused meals is tough if you're haunted by the memory of boiled-to-death Brussels sprouts; limp, canned vegetables; or bitter, soggy eggplant. Given what happens when vegetables are poorly cooked and seasoned, it's no surprise there are a lot of haters. But if you maximize their natural flavors through a few simple techniques like those here, vegetables can transform from being an unfortu-nate necessity of life into something undeniably delicious. Roasting brings out the best in just about all vegetables, intensifying their flavor and releas-ing their natural sweetness to create a caramelized exterior. Braising gives you perfectly tender, richly satisfying vegetables, and sautéing with aromatic herbs is a great way to add layers of fla-vor to a pureed vegetable soup.

A quick note on shopping: For cost and convenience reasons, I'm all for frozen vegetables. We keep broccoli, peas, string beans, spinach, and carrots in the freezer and toss them into quick meals. They're usually flash-frozen within a day or two of harvesting, so flavor and nutrition are still near their peak. There's definitely a difference in texture, though, so I opt to stick with whatever is in season and use frozen vegetables as a backup. Try shopping for produce at markets driven by local farms: Vegetables invariably taste bet-ter and have more nutrients when they are locally grown, because they haven't spent days or weeks traveling to your store. The naturally occurring sugars are at their highest levels when served up fresh—a bonus if you're trying to get kids on the vegetable bandwagon. My daughter goes nuts for the super-sweet crunch of local string beans and chomps on them the whole way home from the farmers' market.

GARLICKY BRUSSELS SPROUTS SERVES 4

This method of making crispy, golden brown–crusted sprouts reveals a level of deep, nutty flavor that scores a lot of points with Brussels sprout lovers (and anyone scarred by encounters with mushy, boiled versions). Cook Brussels sprout halves cut-side down in a super hot pan to work up those irresistible crusts, then flip them one by one. This seems fussy, but it takes all of about 40 seconds to help ensure the even browning you want. In the last minute of cooking, dried oregano, red pepper flakes, and vinegar join in for an easy-to-master, high-fiber dish. The garlic is there to infuse the oil, so I usually discard the cloves after cooking. However, if garlic is your thing, and you're sleeping alone tonight, by all means leave it in. ∎

Adding garlic to a cold pan prevents it from burning and allows its flavor to fully infuse the oil.

4 tablespoons extra virgin olive oil

Fine sea salt and freshly ground black pepper

1 pound Brussels sprouts, trimmed and halved lengthwise (about 2 cups)

3 garlic cloves, peeled and smashed with the flat side of a knife

1 teaspoon dried oregano

Pinch of red pepper flakes

3 tablespoons red wine vinegar

1 Pour 3 tablespoons of the olive oil into a cold 12-inch skillet, add a pinch of salt, and swirl the oil around to coat the pan. Arrange the sprouts cut-side down in one tightly packed layer, and nestle the garlic cloves in between the sprouts. (If everything doesn't fit in one layer, cook the sprouts in batches.)

2 Turn the heat to high, sprinkle with salt and black pepper, and cook for 7 minutes, untouched. They're ready to flip when the cut sides touching the pan have a dark brown crust. Check a couple of sprouts and, if ready, flip each sprout and garlic clove one by one. If they're not there yet, continue cooking for 2 minutes more.

3 Add the remaining 1 tablespoon olive oil to the pan, reduce the heat to medium, and cook for 3 minutes. Add the oregano and pepper flakes and toss with the sprouts and garlic. Add the vinegar and toss again. Cook until the sizzle dies down, about 30 seconds. Taste and adjust the seasoning. Serve warm.

PLANT POWER

Why Vegetables are Vital

It's hard to go a week without hearing about the latest and greatest superfood discovery—some energy-boosting, weight-loss-friendly seed or berry from a faraway mountaintop. While I'm not denying that they're nutritious, there's nothing magical about foods like açai berries and pomegranates. They have more marketing dollars working for them, but they're not healthier than the asparagus or apples at your local farmers' market.

The truth is that every whole plant food is a superfood, and not any one of them can be singled out as the golden ticket to good health. It's their collective powers, the tried-and-true practice of "eating the rainbow" of brightly colored vegetables and fruits, that can steer you away from high blood pressure, heart disease, cancer, and premature aging. By mixing it up in the produce section, you'll not only have far more exciting meals, you'll also benefit from a wider variety of vitamins, minerals, and phytonutrients, the compounds that give plant foods their characteristic colors.

Don't think you can take a one-a-day pill, go right on eating crappy food, and still be fine. Supplements can't capture all the goodness of vitamins and antioxidants in whole foods. The phytonutrients in each fruit and vegetable work as a team, so extracting just one component doesn't cut it.

Many phytochemicals function as antioxidants, including the carotenoids in sweet potatoes, carrots, and butternut squash and the flavonoids in blueberries, grapes, and red wine.

Antioxidants are superheroes that wipe out free radicals—unstable oxygen molecules that damage healthy cells through a process called oxidative stress. Some oxidative stress is normal, but we drastically accelerate it through smoking cigarettes, living in a state of constant stress, and eating shitty acid-forming processed foods. Antioxidants and the plant foods that carry them are crucial because they neutralize free radicals and stop the downward spiral of oxidative stress, ultimately slowing the aging process and reducing the risk of winding up with cancer or a chronic disease like Alzheimer's. So while eating your vegetables doesn't make a miracle cure, it sure as hell makes it a lot less likely that you'll be diagnosed with something truly destructive.

A big source of free radicals is exposure to pesticides and toxins. Some exposure is inevitable, since we live in the modern world, but you can reduce it by buying local or organic produce whenever possible. Buying organic isn't about getting more nutrients, it's about what you're *not* getting: pesticides, fertilizers, fungicides, and other freaky chemicals. Organic options can be pricey, but I consider it a worthwhile investment. Check out the Environmental Working Group's Dirty Dozen list online. If anything on the list is regularly in your shopping cart, you can try to buy the organic version of those. Sometimes, small producers at local farmers' markets use organic practices but haven't gone through the (pricey) official certification. Produce from those farms may be more affordable.

SWEET PEPPER PEPERONATA SERVES 4 TO 6

This exemplifies the simple, delicious Tuscan food I grew up eating. I make it year-round, but it's especially good from late summer to early fall, when antioxidant-rich peppers are prime time. The colorful mix of stewed sweet peppers and onions is great as a condiment with cheese and charcuterie, a filling for an omelet, or a topping heaped on a piece of roasted fish or Flavor-Pounded Chicken (page 213). It also holds its own as a side dish, whether hot out of the pan or served room temperature. Peperonata is even better a few days after making it, so this one is a go-to of mine when I'm cooking for a group and want a few make-ahead dishes. ∎

If you like to flip food around a lot while it cooks, this recipe is an exercise in self-restraint. With too much fiddling that deep browning won't happen, so go easy on it—nurture the browning.

2 garlic cloves, peeled

¼ cup plus 1 tablespoon extra virgin olive oil

1 olive oil–packed brown anchovy fillet, minced

2 large red bell peppers, cut into 1-inch squares

2 large yellow bell peppers, cut into 1-inch squares

1 medium red onion, cut into ½-inch dice

Fine sea salt and freshly ground black pepper

1 cup loosely packed fresh basil leaves, roughly torn

1 tablespoon balsamic vinegar

1 Crack the garlic cloves by giving each one a tap with the flat side of a knife until they split open. In a large, cold high-sided pan, combine ¼ cup of the olive oil, the garlic, and anchovy, then crank the heat to high. When the oil is hot and you see the first wisps of smoke coming off the pan, add the bell peppers (so they get the most heat), then the onion, and season with salt and black pepper. Let the vegetables do their thing in the oil without stirring for about 4 minutes.

2 Stir briefly and let cook for 2 minutes before stirring again. After another minute, or when the pan starts to look dry, add the remaining 1 tablespoon olive oil and stir to coat. Cook until the peppers and onion show browning around the edges and have shrunk down some, about 3 minutes.

3 Reduce the heat to medium-high. Taste and add more salt and pepper, if needed. Cook for 5 minutes, tossing occasionally. Add the basil and continue cooking for 10 minutes, tossing every couple of minutes.

4 Remove the pan from the heat and stir in the vinegar. Serve immediately, or let it come to room temperature and store in the refrigerator.

ROASTED ASPARAGUS AND LEMON WITH CHUNKY PESTO SERVES 4

Freshly roasted asparagus doesn't need much more than good-quality olive oil and salt, but I'm a firm believer that pesto makes everything better. By hand-chopping pesto rather than whizzing it up in a food processor, you get more substantial bits of cheese and pine nuts in every bite. For attractiveness and brightness, I often throw in thin lemon slices with whatever I'm roasting. The heat mellows their acidity and softens the peel so you can eat the slices whole. Avoid using skinny asparagus when roasting, since those can get stringy and burn quickly. ∎

1 bunch medium asparagus

1 tablespoon extra virgin olive oil, plus more for drizzling

1 lemon—½ cut into thin slices, ½ reserved for serving

Fine sea salt and freshly ground black pepper

1 (3-inch) chunk Parmigiano-Reggiano cheese

2 tablespoons pine nuts

½ cup loosely packed fresh basil leaves, coarsely chopped

1 Preheat the oven to 450°F. Line a baking sheet with foil.

2 Trim the asparagus by holding each stalk horizontally and bending until the tough, woody end snaps off. On the baking sheet, toss the asparagus with the olive oil, lemon slices, and salt and pepper to taste. Roast until the asparagus is tender and the lemon slices are lightly browned, about 20 minutes.

3 While the asparagus is roasting, use the tines of a fork to crumble the Parmesan into small nuggets, about 2 tablespoons total. Pile the cheese, pine nuts, and basil together on a cutting board and chop until they're well combined but still chunky.

4 Transfer the roasted asparagus and lemon slices to a serving platter, add the chunky pesto, and toss together. Squeeze the juice of the remaining lemon half and top with a drizzle of olive oil.

ROMESCO SAUCE MAKES ABOUT 2 CUPS

Unbelievably rich and vibrant, a jar of this Spanish pestolike sauce doesn't stand a chance of lasting more than 48 hours when I'm around. Its richness comes from the quality fats in almonds, hazelnuts, and olive oil, so I don't feel bad about my habit of hovering over a jar of it with a spoon. Romesco is traditionally made with grilled or roasted red peppers, but I prefer the ease of this stovetop variation. I've scaled this to a big batch, so use it any time you want to add a punch of piquant flavor to steamed or grilled vegetables or fish. It's dynamite as a dip, a condiment for sandwiches, or stirred into a bowl of quinoa or rice. I also scoop it onto Herb-Roasted Spatchcock Chicken (page 216). ■

5 tablespoons extra virgin olive oil

3 red bell peppers, cut into large pieces

Fine sea salt

3 large garlic cloves, sliced

1 teaspoon smoked paprika

½ cup Marcona almonds

½ cup hazelnuts

1 cup canned stewed tomatoes, drained

2 tablespoons sherry vinegar

1 In a large high-sided skillet, heat 3 tablespoons of the olive oil over high heat. When wisps of smoke start coming off the pan, add the bell peppers and a pinch of salt. Cook for 5 minutes, stirring occasionally. Add the garlic and smoked paprika and cook for 2 minutes. Add the almonds and hazelnuts, reduce the heat to medium-high, and cook for 5 minutes, stirring occasionally. Stir in the tomatoes along with another pinch of salt and reduce the heat to medium. Cook for another 5 minutes so all the flavors come together.

2 Transfer the mixture to a food processor and add the vinegar and remaining 2 tablespoons olive oil. Pulse until thoroughly combined, but still coarse. Taste and adjust seasoning, if needed.

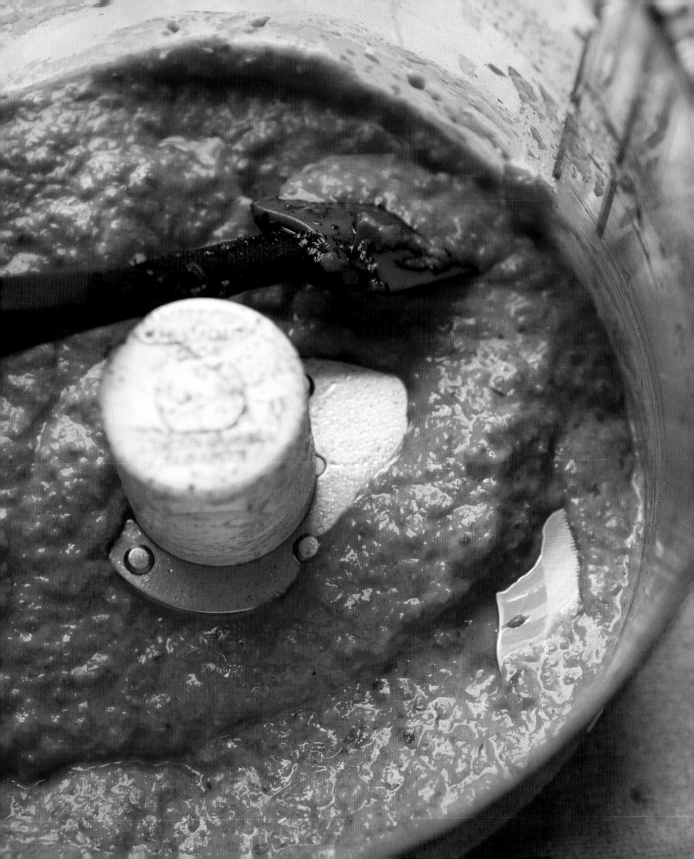

BRAISED STRING BEANS SERVES 6

It's a rare thing when a little effort is rewarded with an impressive result. For this reason, braising is one of my favorite cooking techniques. By doing next to nothing, you get a huge amount of rich flavor. These slow-cooked string beans come out tender and addictively tasty every time (and they're even better the next day, so this is scaled up to give you some leftovers). This will take about 45 minutes to cook, but it's mostly hands off. If you make this during the summer, and I recommend you do, see if you can find Romano beans to sub in for the string beans. They're broader in shape and stand up well to longer cooking like this. If it's the dead of winter and your fresh tomato selection is iffy, feel free to substitute a 28-ounce can of chopped tomatoes. Just be sure to drain the liquid out before adding the tomatoes to the pot. ∎

¼ cup extra virgin olive oil

2 small yellow onions, thinly sliced

1 large garlic clove, peeled and smashed with the flat side of a knife

2 pounds string beans, trimmed and halved crosswise (8 to 9 cups)

6 plum tomatoes, roughly chopped (about 4 cups)

Fine sea salt and freshly ground black pepper

1 cup loosely packed fresh basil leaves, chopped

1 Pour the olive oil into a large cold pot or Dutch oven. Layer in the vegetables—the onions and garlic on the bottom, followed by the string beans and then the tomatoes on top. Add a couple generous pinches of salt and pepper. Cover and turn the heat to high. Cook for 12 minutes, then stir the vegetables to coat them in the liquid they've released. Cover and cook for 3 minutes before stirring again.

2 Reduce the heat to medium and cook for another 5 minutes, then stir and taste. Adjust the seasoning with salt and pepper, if needed. Cover and cook for another 10 minutes. Stir and cook uncovered for 15 minutes, so any remaining liquid evaporates and the flavors concentrate.

3 Add the basil and toss with the string beans. Taste and adjust seasoning.

ROASTED BROCCOLI WITH HAZELNUTS AND PECORINO SERVES 4

Most people typically think of boiling or steaming broccoli, or they have visions of tragic, overcooked broccoli that's limp and awful, and they avoid it altogether. But I think you don't know just how great broccoli can be until you roast it. It becomes tender, while retaining some crispness, and caramelizes to the point where the florets' edges are toasted and crunchy. Toss in hazelnuts, shavings of Pecorino Romano, and a squeeze of lemon, and roasted broccoli becomes addictive. Note to America's parents and school cafeterias: Roast the broccoli and the kids will eat it! The stems are every bit as flavorful and nutritious as the florets, so I like to cut broccoli into spears with a couple of inches of stem on each. ■

1 bunch broccoli

4 tablespoons extra virgin olive oil

Fine sea salt and freshly ground black pepper

¼ cup chopped hazelnuts

Juice of ½ lemon

Chunk of Pecorino Romano cheese, for serving

1 Preheat the oven to 400°F. Line a baking sheet with foil.

2 Cut the broccoli into chunky florets with a few inches of stalk attached.

3 In a large bowl, toss the broccoli with 3 tablespoons of the olive oil and salt and pepper to taste. Spread the broccoli in a single layer on the baking sheet and roast until the edges of the florets are beginning to brown, 20 to 25 minutes. Sprinkle the hazelnuts over the top and roast for 5 minutes more.

4 While the florets are still hot, transfer the broccoli and hazelnuts to a serving bowl and toss with the lemon juice, the remaining 1 tablespoon olive oil, and shaved Pecorino.

LACTO-FERMENTED CARROTS AND GINGER MAKES ABOUT 6 CUPS

Tart and salty with a zing from ginger, I can't get enough of this as a condiment for sandwiches, burgers, and anything spicy. When I stop myself from eating it straight out of the jar, I use a cup of it to make a tangy vinaigrette for salads (page 60). The steps seem long, but the process is pretty straightforward, and naturally occurring good bacteria do most of the work. The key to fermenting success is keeping oxygen exposure to a minimum: The good bacteria hate air, so the carrots and ginger should be fully covered with brine throughout the entire process. Otherwise, mold can develop and spoil the ferment. Faint hissing and popping noises are completely normal, as is the thin, white film that may form on the surface—that's just the friendly probiotics at work. ∎

2 pounds carrots, scrubbed and top ends trimmed
¼ pound fresh ginger, peeled
2 tablespoons fine sea salt

1 In a food processor or on a box grater, shred the carrots and ginger. Combine the shredded vegetables and salt in a large bowl. Knead the mixture like dough, pressing and squeezing it for about 3 minutes to release the natural juices from the carrots and create the brine.

2 Transfer the vegetables and juice to a 2-quart wide-mouth glass jar. Pack the carrots and ginger down into the jar as tightly as possible, using a meat tenderizer or your fist, until the liquid is at least ¼ inch above the carrots. If needed, add a bit of salted water to make sure the vegetables are covered. (There should also be at least 1 inch of space between the top of the liquid and the top of the jar, in case there's spillover during the ferment.) Using a rubber spatula, brush down any bits of carrot or ginger that are stuck to the sides of the jar.

3 Weight down the shredded vegetables in the brine by placing a small circular plastic lid directly on top of them. Place a small saucer over the mouth of the jar. (Using a saucer instead of screwing on the jar's lid allows the gasses produced by the fermentation process to have a way out.)

4 Set aside at room temperature away from direct sunlight to ferment. Keep an eye on it for the first day, checking to make sure the vegetables are still fully submerged. If they're peeking above the liquid, add salted water by the tablespoon until the vegetables are submerged again (avoid stirring up the brine since this could introduce air). Ferment for 5 to 10 days—start your daily tasting on day 5. Once the carrots and ginger reach a level of tangy sourness you like, remove the weight from inside the jar, screw on a lid, and store in the refrigerator. It will keep for months in the fridge.

THE PROBIOTIC POWER OF FERMENTED FOODS

You've heard of probiotics—you can't watch TV, grocery shop, or otherwise live a day in America without seeing a food, pill, or beverage that promises the benefits of probiotics. Probiotics aid a healthy digestive system by restoring and maintaining a healthy balance of gut flora—the hundreds of different sickness-curing and sickness-causing bacteria that constantly battle it out in your gastrointestinal tract. When probiotics, a form of "good" bacteria, are abundant in your body, it's harder for harmful bacteria to take over and make you sick. Those good guys can prevent digestive upset (burps, bloating, and worse) and support your overall immune system.

The most natural way to get the benefits of probiotics is through a variety of lacto-fermented foods. Yogurt, the probiotic poster child, is a fermented milk product, and health food joints are pushing a fizzy, fermented tea called kombucha. I happen to love fermented vegetables. I go for sauerkraut and its Asian cousin, kimchi—both are fermented cabbage—and I'm wild about the lacto-fermented ginger carrots from Hawthorne Valley Farm in New York, which inspired my version here (opposite).

Lacto-fermenting vegetables sounds like it would be a complicated process, and one that involves milk—neither is true. It's basically vegetables in a salty brine left to sit out at room temperature so that beneficial lactic acid bacteria develop ("lacto" refers to *Lactobacillus*, the official name of the bacteria). Lactic acid is a natural preservative that prevents bad bacteria from invading food. Before refrigeration, traditional cultures relied on fermenting because it was the most practical way to extend their food supply. We now know that this process leads to the jackpot of probiotic benefits, so the incredibly simple and gratifying old-school preparation is gaining in popularity again.

LACTO-FERMENTED NAPA CABBAGE AND ONIONS MAKES ABOUT 6 CUPS

If the term "lacto-fermented" is throwing you off, rest assured you're familiar with this one: It's sauerkraut. Cabbage is the most common fermented vegetable and makes a great side dish for cooked meats or a condiment for rich stews. Caraway seeds are the traditional choice for sauerkraut, but you could also use cumin seeds, dill seeds, or celery seeds. ■

1 large head Napa cabbage (about 3 pounds), thinly sliced

1 large yellow onion, thinly sliced

2 tablespoons fine sea salt

1 tablespoon caraway seeds

1 Discard any wilted outer leaves of the cabbage. Core and slice the cabbage into quarters, then thinly slice the cabbage and combine it with the onions, salt, and caraway seeds in a large bowl. Massage the mixture, pressing and squeezing it for about 3 minutes, so the salt pulls water out of the cabbage and creates the brine.

2 Pack the vegetables and any liquid released from the cabbage into a 2-quart wide-mouth glass jar. Press the cabbage into the jar with your fist until it's submerged by about ¼ inch of liquid. (If needed, add a bit of salted water to make sure the vegetables are covered.) Weight the vegetables down in the brine by placing a small plate or circular plastic lid directly on top of the cabbage inside the jar. Cover the mouth of the jar with a small saucer. Set aside at room temperature away from direct sunlight to ferment.

3 On the first day, check the ferment periodically to make sure the vegetables are still fully submerged. If they're poking out of the brine, press down on the plate or lid until the cabbage is submerged again. Add salted water by the tablespoon, if additional liquid is needed.

4 Start tasting the cabbage daily on day 5. Once it tastes sufficiently tangy to you, remove the weight from inside the jar, screw on a lid, and refrigerate. It will keep for months in the fridge.

CREAM-FREE CREAMED CORN SERVES 6

When it's in season, locally grown sweet corn is as good as gold straight off the cob. But for corn-based comfort food, creamed corn is unbeatable. To max out the corn flavor, skip the heavy cream and use the corn itself to provide creaminess. I puree half the kernels to release their natural sweet starches and use this corn "cream" to thicken a mixture of onions and whole corn kernels. It's incredibly good. ■

Here's how I remove corn kernels from the cob without them flying around and ending up on the floor: Lay the cob on a cutting board and cut horizontally from the tip to the end, removing about three rows. Rotate the cob so it rests on the flat side, and remove three more rows. Continue rotating and cutting until all the kernels are removed.

10 ears white corn, shucked

2 tablespoons extra virgin olive oil

1 small yellow onion, diced

Fine sea salt and freshly ground black pepper

2 teaspoons roughly chopped fresh basil

1 Cut the corn kernels from the cobs.

2 In a large high-sided skillet, heat the olive oil over medium heat. Add the onion and salt and pepper to taste. Cook until the onion begins to soften, about 10 minutes. Add the corn kernels, another pinch of salt, and ½ cup water. Cook, stirring occasionally, until the corn is almost tender, about 7 minutes.

3 Transfer half of the corn and onion mixture to a blender and process until smooth. Remove the skillet from the heat and stir in the corn puree. Add the basil and season with salt and pepper to taste.

ROSEMARY SWEET POTATO FRIES SERVES 4

Moments after these fries come out of the oven, we're plucking them off the pan by the handful. I honestly think they've never made it to a plate in our house, even when we double the recipe. Before you jump into this one, banish all notions of classic crispy deep-fried potatoes. Sweet potatoes have a higher water content, so they don't crisp up the way regular potatoes do, but that's exactly why I love them as baked fries. Some turn out super crispy all over, some are soft and a bit floppy, and others have the perfect crunchy, dark brown edges with tender centers. It's the combination of all those irregular textures that makes these so good. ∎

Sweet potatoes are higher in fiber and lower on the glycemic index than regular potatoes, and their bright orange flesh signals a ton of the antioxidant beta-carotene, which converts to vitamin A in the body. The antioxidant activity in sweet potatoes is highest in the skin, so I don't peel them.

1 pound sweet potatoes

3 tablespoons extra virgin olive oil

2 tablespoons fresh rosemary leaves

Fine sea salt and freshly ground black pepper

1 Preheat the oven to 400°F. Line a baking sheet with foil.

2 Scrub the potatoes and pat them dry. Halve each sweet potato crosswise, then lengthwise into sticks about ¼ inch wide (don't be a slave to perfection here; roughly the same size is fine). On the baking sheet, toss the sweet potatoes with the olive oil. Add the rosemary and several pinches of salt and pepper and toss again to coat the fries.

3 Bake for 20 minutes, then gently flip the fries with a spatula. (They will be soft and soggy, so be careful not to mangle them as you flip them over.) Rotate the pan and bake for 15 minutes. Stir once then bake for another 10 minutes or until the fries are nicely browned on the edges and tender in the middle. Loosen them carefully from the pan so you don't rip the foil or the fries.

MAPLE AND SPICE-ROASTED AUTUMN SQUASH SERVES 4 TO 6

This is a version of a popular salad we serve at Hearth. Cubes of tender roasted butternut, red kuri, and kabocha squash are sweetened with just enough maple syrup to balance the spicy warmth of ginger, cinnamon, and nutmeg. I like buttery red kuri squash with the sweeter butternut and creamy kabocha, but any combination of fall squash works. I leave the skins on the kabocha and red kuri squash because they're completely edible and add more fiber and a contrasting texture. Be sure to clean the skin well with a vegetable brush or the coarse side of a clean sponge, and thoroughly scrape out the squash guts and seeds with the edge of a spoon until there are no loose bits. Cut and roast the remaining halves of the kabocha and butternut squash to keep around as snacks or to throw in whatever salad or soup you like. ∎

You've got to get kabocha in your repertoire; its flesh is a silkier, slightly sweeter version of butternut squash. You should be able to find it in your local grocery store during fall and winter, but if not, use acorn squash or just double up on the butternut or red kuri.

½ kabocha squash, 1 red kuri squash, ½ peeled butternut squash, all cut into 1½-inch cubes (about 8 cups cubed squash total)

1½ tablespoons maple syrup

1 teaspoon ground ginger

¾ teaspoon ground cinnamon

¼ teaspoon ground cloves

¼ teaspoon freshly grated nutmeg

1 teaspoon fine sea salt

1½ tablespoons Maple Syrup Vinaigrette (page 58)

Spiced Pumpkin Seeds (page 235), for garnish

1 Preheat the oven to 325°F.

2 In a large bowl, combine the assorted squash cubes and maple syrup. Season with the ginger, cinnamon, cloves, nutmeg, and salt and toss to evenly coat. Arrange the squash on a rimmed baking sheet in a single layer. Cover the pan with foil to help the squash to cook in its own steam and become more infused with the spices. Bake until the squash is soft, about 35 minutes.

3 Remove the squash from the oven, and set aside to cool for 10 minutes, still covered with the foil.

4 While the squash is still warm, transfer it to a large bowl. Add the vinaigrette and lightly toss; don't rough it up too much and break down the squash. Add salt to taste and top each serving with a sprinkling of spiced pumpkin seeds.

KABOCHA
SQUASH

RED KURI
SQUASH

DELICATA
SQUASH

BUTTERNUT
SQUASH

HOW TO CUT WHOLE SQUASH

Instinct tells you to use a giant cleaver and brute force to hack away at it. Don't. There's an easy, effective way that's less likely to involve a 911 call. Start by using a small, sharp knife, rather than a big one; you'll have far more control. Lay the squash on its side on a stable cutting board. You're going to cut it through the equator, rotating as you go.

Kabocha, red kuri, or Delicata (Carnival) squash: Pierce a knife in the center at the equator so the whole blade is in, push down, and rotate the squash. Push down again and rotate. Continue pushing the knife down and rotating the squash until it's fully cut in half. Cut the halves lengthwise into strips of the width you want (for this salad, 1½ inches), then crosswise into cubes.

Butternut squash: Cut the squash in half where the round bulbous part meets the long section. Carefully peel the skin off the long section using a knife first. Then use a vegetable peeler to remove any of the remaining bits of skin and pale yellow flesh. You should see only orange flesh. Halve the long section lengthwise. Lay the halves flat side down and cut lengthwise into strips, then crosswise into cubes. For the bulb, peel it and halve it lengthwise. Scoop out the guts and seeds, place each bulb flat-side down, and cut lengthwise into strips, then crosswise into cubes.

STRAWBERRY AND TOMATO GAZPACHO SERVES 4

In the middle of the summer, right when New York starts to get sticky-hot and cold soup sounds especially good, late strawberry season and early tomato season collide at the market. Inevitably, the two fruits (yep, tomatoes are fruits) end up together in my blender to make this delicious gazpacho. Strawberries seem like the odd man out here, but their sweetness and bit of acidity bring balance to the soup. ∎

3 cups cherry tomatoes

1 pound strawberries, hulled and quartered (about 2 cups); reserve 8 quarters for serving

1 cup peeled, chopped cucumber

1 cup chopped red bell pepper

2 garlic cloves, peeled and smashed with the flat side of a knife

¾ cup extra virgin olive oil, plus more for serving

1 tablespoon plus 1 teaspoon sherry vinegar

Fine sea salt

Fresh basil leaves, torn, for serving

1 In a blender, combine the tomatoes, strawberries, cucumber, bell pepper, garlic, olive oil, vinegar, and a couple pinches of salt and puree until smooth. Taste and adjust seasoning, if needed.

2 Pour the gazpacho into a large bowl or, for a super smooth gazpacho, strain it through a fine-mesh sieve set over a large bowl. Refrigerate until chilled.

3 To serve, ladle the gazpacho into bowls. Chop the reserved strawberries and top each serving of soup with the berries, torn basil, and a drizzle of olive oil.

CARAMELIZED CAULIFLOWER AND APPLE SOUP SERVES 6 TO 8

I've kicked off several Thanksgiving meals with this soup and can confirm that it wins over a wide audience, even the picky people. Pan-roasting the cauliflower in a hot pan brings out its natural sugars and gives it a much deeper flavor. To nail this, be sure that the oil is really hot before adding the vegetables and that you maintain the heat by adding the cauliflower and onions to the pot in several stages, rather than all at once. Without adequate heat, the vegetables will start to release liquid and steam instead of brown. I process the soup in a regular blender, but you could use an immersion blender if you prefer a chunkier consistency. Or if you want super-refined smoothness, you could run the processed soup through a fine-mesh sieve. Subbing in sliced fennel for the cauliflower makes an equally flavorful soup. Either way, this soup is freezer-friendly. ∎

¼ cup extra virgin olive oil

1 large onion, roughly chopped (about 2 cups)

1 large head cauliflower, cut into bite-size pieces, stems included (about 5 cups)

Fine sea salt

2 apples, quartered and cut into 1-inch chunks

2 (4-inch) sprigs of fresh rosemary, folded in half and tied with kitchen twine

½ cup nonalcoholic apple cider

Dehydrated apple chips and chopped walnuts (optional)

1 In a large heavy-bottomed pot or Dutch oven, heat the oil over high heat. When wisps of smoke come off the surface, add one-third of the onion and cauliflower at a time, waiting 1 minute between each addition, then add 2 generous pinches of salt. There should be some serious sizzling sounds, but don't stir just yet—let the florets brown and start to caramelize. After 3 minutes, give it a stir. Cook for 5 minutes, until the vegetables have cooked down by a third. Reduce the heat to medium-high and stir. Cook for 5 minutes, stirring every minute.

2 Add the apples and tied rosemary sprigs. Cover the pot, reduce the heat to low, and simmer for 15 minutes, stirring occasionally.

3 Add the apple cider and 2½ cups water. Cover and bring to a boil over high heat. Reduce the heat and let it simmer for 15 minutes.

4 Working in batches, process the mixture in a blender until smooth. As each batch is blended, pour into another pot over medium heat. Once it's all in, adjust the consistency by adding more water, if you like. Salt to taste. Ladle into bowls and top each serving with a sprinkling of crumbled apple chips and chopped walnuts, if desired.

MOROCCAN-SPICED EGGPLANT SOUP SERVES 6 TO 8

This soup feels decadent because of how silky and luxuriously creamy it is. You'd think it'd been bombed with a ton of oil or cream, but the richness is all in the texture of the eggplant and the addition of almond milk and a little Greek yogurt. I typically use the Italian or globe varieties when I roast, fry, or bread eggplant. Here, I go for the smaller Japanese eggplants, which have fewer, smaller seeds and a sweeter, more delicate flavor. Serving the soup with a spoonful of vinegar-soaked raisins provides some acidity and a pop of texture. ∎

¼ cup extra virgin olive oil

2 small yellow onions, chopped

1½ teaspoons ground cinnamon

2½ teaspoons ground cumin

2 teaspoons ground ginger

1 teaspoon turmeric

5 large Japanese eggplants, peeled and chopped (about 8 cups)

Fine sea salt

2 cups unsweetened almond milk

½ cup golden raisins

1 tablespoon white wine vinegar

¼ cup full-fat plain Greek yogurt plus 2 tablespoons, for serving

½ cup sliced almonds, toasted

1 In a large pot, combine the olive oil and onions, then turn the heat to medium-high. When the onions start to sizzle, reduce the heat to medium-low. Add the cinnamon, cumin, ginger, and turmeric and stir to coat the onions with the spices. Cover and cook, stirring occasionally, until the onions are translucent, about 15 minutes.

2 Add the eggplants and a couple pinches of salt to the pot and stir to thoroughly combine with the onions. Cover and increase the heat to medium. Cook, stirring every few minutes, until the eggplant is softened and its volume has shrunk in half, about 15 minutes.

3 Add the almond milk and 2 cups water. Bring to a boil over high heat, then reduce the heat to low and simmer for 30 minutes.

4 While the soup simmers, reconstitute the raisins. In a small bowl, combine the raisins and vinegar. Add enough warm water to cover by about ¼ inch. Set aside.

5 Working in batches if necessary, pour the soup into a blender. Add the yogurt and process until smooth. Taste and adjust the seasoning. Ladle into bowls and garnish with the sliced almonds, vinegar-soaked raisins, and dollops of Greek yogurt.

JAPANESE SWEET POTATO AND CAULIFLOWER FRITTATA SERVES 6 TO 8

Frittatas allow you to turn a pile of vegetables into a really filling meal, so this is a great dish to have in your bag of tricks. (This is an extra-large frittata, but trust me—you want leftovers. Frittata cold out of the fridge is just as good as hot out of the pan.) I like the vegetables to dominate more than the egg, and this particularly hearty version gets its flavor from pan-roasting cauliflower and Japanese sweet potatoes until they're soft and caramelized. As far as technique, I find that the conventional route of starting a frittata on the stovetop and finishing it in the oven is a total sham. Either it comes out overcooked and dense, or the top doesn't brown. I cook a frittata start-to-finish on the stove, so it gets nicely browned on both sides. It's a little trickier (and some would say more stressful) because you have to flip it and slip it back into the pan, but that extra effort is rewarded with a more flavorful, lighter frittata. If you're nervous about it, do the flip over the sink. Once you ace this technique, you can improvise the filling based on the vegetables you have around. ∎

7 tablespoons extra virgin olive oil, plus more if needed

1 small head cauliflower, cut into small florets (about 3 cups)

2 Japanese sweet potatoes, halved lengthwise and cut into ¼-inch-thick slices (about 3 cups)

1 medium white onion, sliced (about 1½ cups)

Fine sea salt and freshly ground black pepper

8 large eggs

¼ cup whole milk

¼ cup freshly grated Parmigiano-Reggiano cheese

½ cup coarsely chopped fresh flat-leaf parsley

1 In a 12-inch nonstick skillet, heat 3 tablespoons of the olive oil over high heat until it starts to smoke. Combine the cauliflower and sweet potatoes in a tightly packed layer to fill the bottom of the pan. Scatter the onion on top and cook for 1 minute without stirring.

2 Reduce the heat to medium-high. Add 2 big pinches of salt and a few grinds of pepper and cook for 3 minutes. Stir the vegetables and cook, stirring occasionally, until they are nicely browned, about 7 minutes.

If the pan seems dry, add 1 teaspoon olive oil. Reduce the heat to medium, cover, and cook, stirring a couple of times, until the vegetables have softened, about 15 minutes.

3 While the filling cooks, make the base. In a bowl, whisk the eggs, milk, 3 tablespoons of the olive oil, Parmesan, and parsley. Season with salt and pepper.

4 Uncover the skillet and add salt and pepper to taste. Move the vegetables around so they fill the pan in an even layer. Drizzle the remaining 1 tablespoon olive oil around the perimeter of the pan. Crank the heat to high.

5 Pour the egg mixture over the vegetables. After 1 minute, reduce the heat to medium. As the egg starts to set, use a spatula to pull the edges away from the rim of the pan and poke holes across the center, letting raw egg fill in around the cooked vegetables. Adjust the heat, if needed, so the eggs are lightly bubbling. Continue to gently lift the edges of the frittata and tilt the pan, so uncooked egg seeps underneath. Cook until there's almost no runny egg, 5 to 6 minutes.

6 Prepare to flip by running a spatula around the edges, loosening the egg from the pan. To make sure it is not sticking, give the pan a shake. The frittata should move as a whole. (If it sticks, remove the pan from the heat and let it set for 3 minutes, then use the spatula to loosen the frittata from the pan.)

7 Put a large plate over the skillet and turn the frittata over onto the plate. Slide the frittata back into the pan and cook the other side over medium heat for 2 minutes. Run the spatula around the edge again and flip the frittata onto a serving plate. Let it rest for 5 minutes. Cut and serve warm or at room temperature.

Japanese sweet potatoes are burgundy-skinned beauties with off-white flesh that tastes more like a chestnut than a sweet potato. I prefer the drier flesh of the Japanese variety here, but you can swap in regular sweet potatoes.

BEANS & LENTILS

MY MOM IS FROM TUSCANY, LAND of the "bean-eaters" in Italy, so I grew up eating loads of beans. Cannellini, chickpeas, and borlotti (cranberry beans) are key players in just about every classic Tuscan meal, so I naturally lean toward these. Good thing too, since eating the occasional bowl of warm, just-cooked beans or ribollita was one of the few things I actually did right in my old diet. Beans pack a punch of fiber, and they're a great non-meat source of protein. Factor in that they're affordable, readily available, and versatile, and you've got one of the most perfect foods.

They've gone from making an occasional appearance to being a full-time kitchen staple. My wife, Amanda, makes a pot of beans most Sundays, changing up the bean of choice each time, and we turn them into various dishes—salads, soups, dips, you name it. I treat them as more than simple fillers—their creamy texture, robust flavor, and richness are often the focus of my meals. A pot of lentils leads to a soul-warming Lentil Soup with Tomato and Tuscan Kale (page 122), chickpeas become a main-course salad punched up with white anchovies and pickled onions (page 127), and velvety cannellini beans get an *ucceletto* treatment of tomatoes and Tuscan herbs (page 117).

Many of the recipes here make a large quantity. My thinking on beans and bean soups is that if you're going to make them, make a big batch. Unlike meat or fish, very little extra effort is needed to make a bean recipe that serves 8 instead of 4. Also, beans are great freezer food. Generally, I find that the simple process of cooking dried beans results in far better flavor and denser texture than canned beans because you control the salt and cooking time. Canned beans are typically overcooked to the point of falling apart, and that thick, goopy canned bean slime is nasty. Any time you use store-bought beans, buy the low-sodium or no-salt-added varieties, drain, and thoroughly rinse the beans before cooking. Getting on the dried bean bandwagon calls for conquering any intimidation or confusion, so here are my tips to turning out a killer pot of beans:

1 Start with fresh, good-quality dried beans. The fresher they are, the faster and more evenly they cook. It's almost impossible to identify a fresh dried bean, so it's helpful to look into the habits of the brand or supplier of beans you buy. I like Rancho Gordo because they grow and dry their beans in small quantities and include an expiration date.

2 When soaking beans overnight, be sure to cover the beans with water so there are several inches of liquid above the beans. If some beans are sticking out above the waterline the next day, it's a sign that not enough water was added, and there's no way the beans are going to cook evenly.

3 Cook beans in a heavy pot covered by an inch or so of water. Heavy pots diffuse heat better so your beans will cook more evenly.

4 Think of the liquid you cook beans in as a blank canvas. Water and stock work equally well. If you want to flavor the liquid, throw in half an onion or some garlic cloves, chopped carrot or celery.

5 The big debate is when to salt the beans. I used to do it when the beans were almost done cooking, but now I soak the dried beans in salted water. As the beans absorb the liquid, they take in the salt. This method gives you a superior pot of evenly salted, flavorful beans with soft skins.

6 Store cooked leftover beans in some of their cooking liquid—enough to barely cover them. This prevents the skins from drying out and cracking. Also, several recipes here call for some of the bean cooking liquid, which acts as a flavorful thickener.

Whenever I cook a pot of beans, I always have a bowl as soon as they're done. There's nothing like a bowl of just-cooked chickpeas dressed while they're hot with really good olive oil, sea salt, and freshly cracked black pepper. I highly recommend trying this with any bean or lentil you make. Bean nirvana.

POT OF BEANS MAKES 6 CUPS

Making homemade beans is hardly laborious; it just requires a little foresight. Some say it's unnecessary, but I find soaking dried beans before cooking them is essential to a shorter cooking time (not to mention easing beans' notoriously noisy side effect). An overnight soak is ideal, but the quick-soak method noted here is good in a pinch. The time it takes to cook a pot of beans can take anywhere from 45 minutes to upwards of 2 hours depending on the type, size, and age of the bean you're cooking (chickpeas in particular take a while). The method will always be the same, though, so you can use this recipe for any variety of dried bean. I just happen to use cannellini beans the most, in no small part because of Ucceletto Beans (page 117) and Ribollita (page 119). ■

My quick-soak method: Add the beans to a large pot and cover them with water by 4 inches. Salt the water, cover the pot, and bring to a boil over high heat. As soon as it reaches a boil, remove from the heat and let sit for 1 hour covered. Drain and rinse.

1 pound dried cannellini beans (or any dried bean)

Fine sea salt

1 head garlic

1 bunch fresh sage

Extra virgin olive oil (optional)

Freshly cracked black pepper (optional)

1 Add the beans to a large bowl and cover them with water by at least 4 inches. Add enough salt so the water tastes like the sea. Let sit overnight (at least 12 hours) at room temperature.

2 The next day, drain the beans, put them in a very large pot, and add enough water to cover them by about 2 inches. Remove any loose, papery outer layers from the head of garlic and cut off about ¼ inch of the stem end to expose the cloves. Add the head of garlic and the sage to the pot.

3 Cook the beans gently over medium heat, adjusting the temperature so the water bubbles just occasionally. When the beans soften, but are not quite tender, give them a taste. If more salt is needed, add it now so the beans will finish cooking in properly seasoned liquid. Continue cooking until they are soft and creamy. The time will vary, but I start checking them after 30 minutes and generally find that they're done somewhere between 45 minutes and 1 hour 30 minutes.

4 Serve the beans warm with olive oil and black pepper. Or cool the beans, put them in a glass storage container, and add enough of their cooking liquid to fully submerge them. Store them in the refrigerator for up to a week.

FIBER

The Benefits of Roughing It

Until a few years ago, the only time fiber ever crossed my mind was catching a rerun of the classic *Saturday Night Live* commercial for "Colon Blow," a hilarious spoof of high-fiber, sticks-and-twigs-style cereals (if you've never seen this gem, take two minutes to watch it online). Most of us associate fiber with good digestion, but have no clue why it's useful beyond that. I assumed fiber would only be a concern when I was an old man in need of Colon Blow cereal, prunes, and Metamucil.

But fiber's importance became clear to me when I realized that filling up on super delicious, high-fiber foods was a much easier approach to changing my diet than calorie counting and constant hunger. Foods with fiber stabilize blood sugar, digest more slowly, and take up more space in your stomach, so you feel fuller longer. It's tough to gorge on fiber-rich foods (even for people like me who suck at self-restraint), so fiber became my insurance against overeating. To feel satisfied eating low-fiber white bread, sliced deli meat, and cookies, I had to rely on hefty quantities, but I rarely feel the need to double-down on bowls of Warm Lentil Salad (page 130) or Cranberry Bean Soup with Farro (page 120) because their combination of great flavor and high fiber is so gratifying.

Beans are the most naturally rich sources of fiber, but all plant foods have it: vegetables, fruits, whole grains, nuts, and seeds. Fiber is an indigestible carbohydrate that comes in two forms—soluble and insoluble. Insoluble fiber helps to haul out the trash and toxins. It absorbs liquid in your stomach, so it expands and keeps things moving through your digestive tract. Without enough of it, you'd have a seriously uncomfortable pile-up happening. Whole grains, especially intact grains (page 140), leafy greens, and the outer skins of fruits and vegetables are good sources of insoluble fiber (I never peel foods like sweet potatoes or apples for this reason).

Soluble fiber attracts water in your stomach, forming a gel that binds with food, slowing the speed with which it empties from your stomach—this fills you up and delays the absorption of sugar, keeping blood sugar levels steady. You've heard that eating a whole apple is better than drinking the juice? It's because the soluble fiber in the apple's pulp prevents the blood sugar spike and crash that happens if you just have the sugary juice on its own. Foods with soluble fiber—including beans, lentils, oatmeal, and citrus fruits—are also known for reducing LDL (bad) cholesterol levels and lowering chances of a heart attack.

Don't worry about choosing a specific type of fiber—most foods that naturally contain it have both insoluble and soluble. Just be sure you're getting fiber from real, whole foods. Don't rely on packaged foods that advertise "fiber enriched"—this type of added fiber won't squash hunger or cravings, and the processed stuff inevitably comes with questionable ingredients and fewer nutrients than whole foods.

A word to the wise—if beans and other high-fiber foods aren't a regular part of your meals, don't immediately start with big servings of them (unless you're prepared for cramps and frequent trips to the bathroom). Start small, add them in slowly, and drink a ton of water so your body can get used to the increase in fiber. I worked my way up, adding chia seeds to shakes, choosing intact whole grains like quinoa and sweet brown rice instead of white rice, and working more of my favorite classic bean dishes like Ribollita (page 119) and Ucceletto Beans (page 117) into my repertoire. Eating with high-fiber foods in mind takes away the need to think about what foods are "good" or "bad"—anything naturally high in fiber gets a green light. It's that simple.

UCCELETTO BEANS SERVES 6

My annual cooking class at Montecastelli in Italy always kicks off with a quintessential Tuscan feast, and without fail, the knockout dish is *ucceletto* beans with pork sausage. To cook beans *ucceletto*-style is to cook them "in the manner of little birds." It's a reference to sage, rosemary, tomato, and garlic—the ingredients traditionally used to cook squab and quail in Italy. These beans are simple, homey, and pretty glorious. You can easily make this into a one-pan meal by browning a few links of sausage and adding the *ucceletto* beans (cooked with all the juice from the can of tomatoes) to the pan to stew with the sausages. ■

3 tablespoons extra virgin olive oil, plus more for serving

4 garlic cloves, halved lengthwise and thinly sliced (about 1 packed tablespoon)

1 (28-ounce) can whole peeled tomatoes, roughly chopped, half the juice from the can reserved

Fine sea salt and freshly ground black pepper

2 tablespoons finely chopped fresh sage

2 tablespoons finely chopped fresh rosemary

4 cups cooked cannellini beans (page 113), or 2½ (15-ounce) cans cannellini beans, rinsed and drained

¼ cup of bean cooking liquid or water

1 In a cold, large high-sided skillet, combine the olive oil and garlic, then turn the heat to high. As soon as the garlic shows the slightest tinge of brown, about 2 minutes in, stir in the tomatoes and the reserved juice. Add a pinch of salt and cook for 5 minutes to concentrate the flavors and reduce the liquid. Add the sage, rosemary, and a generous amount of pepper and cook for 1 minute.

2 Add the beans and their cooking liquid (or ¼ cup water, if using canned beans). Cook until there's no liquid pooling on the bottom of the pan and the sauce coats and sticks to the beans, about 5 minutes. Serve warm, dressed with pepper and a drizzle of olive oil.

BEANS AND GREENS SERVES 4 TO 6

Due to the dish's simplicity, value, and hearty goodness, virtually every culture I can think of has its own version of beans and greens. The version I know best is Italian-style escarole and cannellini beans, though I often use red kidney beans for their ability to hold their shape and absorb flavors really well. The key ingredients here are the ones you barely notice: Anchovies add the undeniable tastiness of umami (page 149) and the starchy bean liquid helps to bring the beans and tender greens together. Aside from being a speedy dish to put together, it easily adapts to whatever beans and hardy greens you have on hand. Cannellini beans, chickpeas, kale, mustard greens, and dandelion greens have all found their way into this—with great results. ■

2 olive oil–packed anchovy fillets

3 tablespoons extra virgin olive oil, plus more for serving

3 large garlic cloves, thinly sliced

¼ teaspoon red pepper flakes

1 large head escarole, core discarded, leaves washed and coarsely chopped

Fine sea salt and freshly ground black pepper

2 cups cooked red kidney beans (page 113), or 1½ (15-ounce) cans red kidney beans, rinsed and drained

¼ cup of bean cooking liquid or water

Freshly grated Parmigiano-Reggiano cheese, for serving

1 Mince the anchovies and mash into a smooth paste with the flat side of a large heavy knife.

Add it to a large skillet with the olive oil, garlic, and pepper flakes. Turn the heat to medium and cook until the anchovy melts into the oil and the garlic just begins to brown, about 3 minutes. Add the escarole, a pinch of salt, and a few grinds of pepper. Increase the heat to medium-high. Using tongs, toss the greens to coat them in the oil. Cook until the escarole is wilted and has released a bit of liquid in the bottom of the pan, about 5 minutes.

2 Add the kidney beans and their cooking liquid (or water, if using canned beans) and toss. Reduce the heat to medium and simmer until the greens are tender and the liquid is absorbed, about 15 minutes. Taste and adjust the seasoning. Top each serving with black pepper and freshly grated Parmesan.

RIBOLLITA SERVES 8

Another of Hearth's greatest hits and my all-time favorite soup, ribollita is among the first recipes I earmarked for this book. I've waxed poetic about this Tuscan soup for years, but I've recently come to appreciate it as an ideal good food day meal. Ribollita is delicious, hearty perfection—a well-balanced meal of tender vegetables and plump cannellini beans in a thick, hearty soup. It's traditionally made with a lot of bread, but I swap in extra cannellini beans for more heft. I want to take a swan dive into it every time its aroma fills the kitchen. You don't want to hurry this soup along. Stewing the cabbage and kale in their own juices for 20 minutes is a crucial step to developing the deep flavor of good ribollita. You'll be grateful to have leftovers, so make a big pot—it's even better the next day. ∎

To get the Tuscan kale to disperse throughout the soup, it needs to be chopped into very small pieces. You can chop it by hand, but I go an easier route by freezing the bunches of kale overnight. A night in the freezer makes the kale brittle, so you can crumble the leaves into a million pieces. Then just discard the thick center ribs.

2 tablespoons extra virgin olive oil

3 cups diced yellow onions

3 cups diced carrots

3 cups diced celery

Fine sea salt and freshly ground black pepper

1 head savoy cabbage, chopped (about 4 cups)

⅓ cup plus 1 tablespoon tomato paste

4 bunches Tuscan kale, finely chopped or crumbled (about 8 cups; see note)

10 cups Chicken Broth (page 199) or water

5 cups cooked cannellini beans (page 113), or 3½ (15-ounce) cans cannellini beans, rinsed and drained

Freshly grated Parmigiano-Reggiano cheese, for serving

Fresh thyme leaves, for serving

1 In a very large soup pot, heat the olive oil over medium heat. Add the onions, carrots, celery, and a pinch of salt, and stir to coat the vegetables with the oil. Cover and cook the vegetables, stirring occasionally, until they begin to soften but have not developed any browning, about 10 minutes.

2 Stir in the savoy cabbage, cover, and cook until it begins to wilt, about 3 minutes. Add the tomato paste, stirring to combine it with the vegetables. Reduce the heat to low, add the kale, and stir well. Cover the pot and stew the vegetables until they're tender, about 20 minutes. Add the broth or water, increase the heat, and bring the soup to a boil.

3 While the soup is coming to a boil, puree 3 cups of the beans in a blender or food processor, adding a little water if necessary. Whisk the pureed beans into the boiling soup. Add the remaining 2 cups of whole beans and bring the soup back to a boil. Reduce the heat and gently simmer uncovered for about 30 minutes to allow the flavors to come together.

4 Taste and season with salt and lots of pepper. Serve immediately with freshly grated Parmesan and thyme. Cool and refrigerate or freeze any leftovers.

CRANBERRY BEAN SOUP WITH FARRO SERVES 8

To welcome dinner guests at Hearth, everyone is given a shot of soup before their meal, and this amazingly creamy, classic Tuscan bean soup is our late fall and winter offering. The silky texture and deeply satisfying flavor give it a disguise of decadence, though it's really a wholesome, fiber-rich soup of basic ingredients. I'm crazy for varying textures in a dish, so when I make this at home I add cooked grains for a bit of chewiness. I like farro best, but brown rice and barley are good alternatives. As with any pureed soup, this freezes well with no loss of taste or texture. Rather than cut the recipe in half, be kind to your future self and freeze any leftovers in single- or double-serving containers. ■

3 tablespoons extra virgin olive oil, plus more for serving

2 medium onions, chopped (about 2 cups)

3 small carrots, chopped (about 1 cup)

3 celery stalks, chopped (about 1 cup)

8 garlic cloves, peeled and smashed with the flat side of a knife

3 olive oil–packed anchovy fillets

Fine sea salt

1 tablespoon tomato paste

1 pound dried cranberry beans, soaked (using overnight or quick-soak method, page 113) and drained

Bouquet garni (a few sprigs each of fresh thyme, rosemary, and sage, tied together with kitchen twine), plus extra thyme for garnish

1½ cups cooked farro (page 146)

Freshly grated Parmigiano-Reggiano cheese, for serving

1 In a large soup pot, heat the olive oil over high heat. When the oil is hot and slides easily across the pan, add the onions, carrots, celery, garlic, anchovies, and a couple of pinches of salt. Cook, stirring occasionally, until the vegetables are soft and lightly browned, about 10 minutes.

2 Add the tomato paste, stirring well to coat the vegetables. Reduce the heat to medium-low and cook, stirring occasionally, until the mixture has thickened and darkened, about 10 minutes.

3 Stir in the beans, 10 cups water, the bouquet garni, and a couple of pinches of salt. Bring to a boil over high heat, then reduce to a gentle simmer (there should only be a little movement in the liquid). Cook, stirring occasionally, until the beans are soft and creamy, anywhere from 1 to 2 hours. (This is a forgiving soup, so don't worry about overcooking it.)

4 Remove the bouquet garni. Working in batches, puree the soup in a blender and add to another large pot over medium heat. Add salt and pepper to taste and adjust the consistency with more water or broth, if needed.

5 To serve, put 2 generous tablespoons of farro in each serving bowl, ladle a cup of soup over it, and garnish with fresh thyme, freshly grated Parmesan, and a few dots of olive oil.

LENTIL SOUP WITH TOMATO AND TUSCAN KALE SERVES 8 TO 10

This is an unbelievably hearty vegetarian soup for when you go into hibernation mode in the chilly months (and with leftovers that freeze well, you can go out even less). The deep richness of *soffrito* infuses so much flavor, there's no need for broth or meat to make this soup shine. You want a lentil that breaks down a bit, so go with brown lentils rather than French green Puy lentils. The thickness of the soup is a matter of personal preference. I like it thick, so I puree a portion of the lentils and stick to only 2 cups of water added in the end. If a brothy consistency is your thing, skip pureeing the lentils and add more water. ∎

Countless classic Italian soups, stews, and sauces start with the knock-your-socks-off flavor of *soffrito*, minced vegetables softly fried in a generous amount of olive oil. This cornerstone of Italian cooking is usually made of onions, carrots, and either celery or fennel, along with other aromatics (like herbs, tomatoes, and dried peperoncini) that vary depending on what you're making. Make sure the vegetables are minced and that they are fried in sizzling olive oil. The longer *soffrito* cooks, the more color and complexity it develops. It's an incredible flavor booster.

LENTILS

1 head garlic

1 pound brown lentils

½ yellow onion

1 carrot, peeled and halved lengthwise

1 celery stalk, cut into large pieces

1 bay leaf

Fine sea salt

SOFFRITO AND VEGETABLES

1 medium red onion, coarsely chopped (about 2 cups)

2 small carrots, coarsely chopped (about 1 cup)

2 celery stalks, coarsely chopped (about 1 cup)

1 tablespoon fresh rosemary leaves

1 tablespoon fresh thyme leaves

½ cup extra virgin olive oil, plus more for serving

1 tablespoon tomato paste

1 (14.5-ounce) can whole peeled tomatoes with their juices

Fine sea salt and freshly ground black pepper

1 bunch Tuscan kale, stems and center ribs removed, leaves washed and coarsely chopped

Freshly grated Parmigiano-Reggiano cheese, for serving

1 For the lentils: Remove the outer layers from the head of garlic and cut off about ¼ inch of the stem end to expose the cloves. Add the lentils to a large pot and cover them by 2 inches with water. Add the onion, carrot, celery, bay leaf, the head of garlic, and a couple of pinches of salt. Bring the lentils to a boil over high heat, reduce the heat to a simmer, and cook until the lentils are creamy and tender, about 40 minutes.

2 Remove and discard the onion, carrot, celery, bay leaf, and garlic. Using an immersion blender, puree about one-third of the lentils. (Or scoop one-third of the lentils into a standard blender and puree, then add back to the pot.)

3 For the soffrito: In a food processor, combine the red onion, carrots, celery, rosemary, and thyme and pulse until the vegetables are minced. Add the mixture to a separate large soup pot along with the olive oil. Turn the heat to high and fry the vegetables, stirring occasionally, until they soften and color slightly, 10 to 12 minutes.

4 Add the tomato paste, canned tomatoes with their juice, and a couple pinches of salt to the soffrito and stir. Reduce the heat to medium-high and cook for 10 minutes. Add the kale and another pinch of salt, stirring to coat the leaves. Reduce the heat to medium and cook for 10 minutes, until the kale is soft.

5 Pour the lentils into the pot of vegetables and stir. Add about 2 cups water, a little at a time, to thin the soup (it can be more or less water, depending on the level of thickness you prefer). Increase the heat to high and bring to a boil. Reduce the heat and simmer for about 30 minutes to allow the flavors to come together. Taste and add salt, if needed. Serve with black pepper, Parmesan, and a drizzle of olive oil.

CHICKPEA CREPE SANDWICHES WITH ZUCCHINI, TOMATO, AND MOZZARELLA MAKES 4 SANDWICHES

My wife, Amanda, started making gluten-free crepes (recipe follows) as a bread alternative, and I'm nuts for them. They're very similar to *cecina*, a popular Italian street food made of chickpea flour, olive oil, salt, and water. These sturdy crepes are the perfect portable sandwich pockets for lunch or snacks when you're traveling. I've given you my favorite sandwich version here: a combination of sautéed zucchini with tomatoes and mozzarella. ■

4 Chickpea Crepes (recipe follows)

2 tablespoons extra virgin olive oil

3 medium zucchini, sliced into ¼-inch rounds

Fine sea salt and freshly ground black pepper

1 medium onion, sliced

¼ cup coarsely chopped fresh basil

8 slices fresh mozzarella (6 to 8 ounces)

12 cherry tomatoes, halved

1 Make the chickpea crepes.

2 In a large skillet, heat the oil over high heat. When the first wisps of smoke come off the pan, add the zucchini and season with salt and pepper. Pile the onion on top and cook the vegetables without stirring until you begin to see color on the edges of the zucchini, about 2 minutes. Stir and continue cooking until the vegetables are soft and nicely browned, about 10 minutes. Fold in the chopped basil.

3 Top each chickpea crepe with one-fourth of the zucchini mixture, 2 slices of cheese, and a handful of tomatoes. Season with salt and pepper, then fold the crepe around the filling and eat it like a taco.

RECIPE CONTINUES

CHICKPEA CREPES

MAKES ABOUT 5 CREPES

We add arrowroot powder to the crepe batter to create individual 6-inch crepes sturdy enough to hold a combo of veggies, cheese, or scrambled eggs for sandwiches. Occasionally, we punch up the batter with spices and finely chopped herbs (see Variations, at right) and eat the crepes on their own. Make a batch ahead and wrap them in foil until you're ready to reheat them. Or, make the batter and keep in the fridge for up to a week, cooking crepes as needed. ■

2 cups chickpea flour

1 cup arrowroot flour

1 teaspoon fine sea salt

½ teaspoon baking soda

Extra virgin olive oil

1 In a large bowl, whisk together the chickpea flour, arrowroot flour, salt, and baking soda. Whisk in ¾ cup water. Then continue adding water, ¼ cup at a time, whisking between additions, until the batter's consistency is smooth and velvety with no lumps, thinner than pancake batter, but still thick enough to coat a spoon.

2 In a 10-inch skillet, heat 1 teaspoon olive oil over high heat. When the oil moves quickly across the pan, pour ½ cup of batter in the center of the pan. Quickly spread the batter into a thin circle by tilting the pan around in a circular motion or using the back of a spoon. Reduce the heat to medium-high. Cook for about 2 minutes, or until you start to see air bubbles and holes in the crepe. Flip it and cook for another minute. Remove it from the pan. Repeat with more oil and the remaining batter, stacking the finished crepes on a plate as you go.

Variations
- 1 tablespoon finely chopped rosemary and grated zest of 1 small lemon
- Add 1½ teaspoons garam masala to the batter; cook the crepes in virgin coconut oil instead of olive oil
- 1 tablespoon smoked paprika
- 1 tablespoon curry powder
- 2 tablespoons chopped scallions

CHICKPEA AND WHITE ANCHOVY SALAD SERVES 6

Here's one for your next party. This easy, inexpensive bean salad looks awesome piled onto a platter and served family-style with a few whole white anchovy fillets on top. The bright flavors, creamy-crunchy texture, and heartiness fully deliver on its visual promise. This is a large amount, so if you're after a simple lunch to have around for a few days, you can halve the recipe with no issues. Look for marinated white anchovies in the refrigerated cases, often near the cheese and olives. White anchovies are cured in vinegar and taste less intense than the salty oil-packed brown anchovies in a tin. There's no substituting one for the other. ∎

The celery heart is the group of pale green, tender, mildly flavored stalks at the center of the bunch. The leaves on these stalks have a ton of great flavor, so think of them as an herb to chop up and add to salads and soups.

½ red onion, thinly sliced

Fine sea salt and freshly ground black pepper

Red wine vinegar

3 cups cooked chickpeas (page 113) or 2 (15-ounce) cans chickpeas, rinsed and drained

¼ pound marinated white anchovy fillets, drained and cut into ¼-inch chunks (about ½ cup)

1 cup sliced celery heart stalks and leaves

½ cup packed chopped fresh flat-leaf parsley

½ cup thinly sliced radishes (about 5 medium)

¼ cup extra virgin olive oil

1 To pickle the onion, add the slices to a small bowl with a sprinkle of salt and just enough red wine vinegar to cover (about 3 tablespoons). Set aside to pickle for at least 15 minutes.

2 In a large bowl, combine the chickpeas, anchovies, celery, parsley, radishes, and a couple of big pinches of salt and pepper. Add the olive oil and the pickled onions along with their pickling liquid. Toss everything together. Taste and adjust the salt and pepper, if necessary.

**CHICKPEA AND WHITE
ANCHOVY SALAD
(PAGE 127)**

WARM LENTIL SALAD SERVES 8

This is an ideal make-ahead salad, and probably the one I make the most. It has no seasonal boundaries and comes together with little effort, and its rich, earthy flavor is satisfying on every level. I always make a big portion because it holds well in the fridge, but you can easily halve it if you're cooking for one or two. Puy lentils, a small, green French variety, are the most salad-friendly because they retain their shape and firm texture through the cooking process. Brown lentils also work, but yellow and red lentils aren't durable enough and tend to get mushy. This salad is plenty substantial on its own, but that shouldn't stop you from occasionally tossing in a cup of bocconcini, small balls of mozzarella cheese. I also like a bowl of this topped with a piece of seared salmon or draped with a fried egg. ■

Unlike dried beans, lentils don't need presoaking, and they cook quickly—ideal for quick weeknight meals. You can certainly skip the salad ingredients here and keep the simple pot of lentils around for tossing in soups and green salads.

1 pound French green lentils, rinsed

½ white onion, peeled but core intact

3 bay leaves

2 garlic cloves, peeled

1 carrot, peeled and quartered lengthwise

1 tablespoon fine sea salt

2 bunches scallions, white and pale green parts only, thinly sliced

½ cup packed chopped fresh flat-leaf parsley

¼ cup red wine vinegar

¼ cup extra virgin olive oil

Freshly ground black pepper

1 In a large pot, combine the lentils, onion, bay leaves, garlic, carrot, and salt. Cover by 2 inches with cold water and bring to a boil over high heat. Reduce the heat to a simmer and cook until the lentils are tender, but not falling apart, 17 to 20 minutes. Set the pot aside until the lentils are cool enough to handle.

2 Drain the lentils, allowing them to sit in the strainer for a couple of minutes. Remove and toss out the bay leaves, garlic, and onion. Remove the pieces of carrot, slice them, and add to a large bowl along with the scallions, parsley, and drained lentils. Dress with the vinegar and olive oil and toss to combine. Add salt and pepper to taste.

BLACK BEAN DIP MAKES 4 CUPS

Bean dips are creamy by nature, but adding olive oil and avocado results in supreme smoothness and full-bodied flavor. They also lighten the consistency of the dip, making it less grainy and more pliable—no breaking your corn chips in thick, sludgy bean dip. I'm not wild about spicy food, but if you like in-your-face heat, by all means add half a chopped jalapeño, or a few dashes of hot sauce or cayenne pepper. For a little texture contrast, you could garnish this with minced red onion or sliced scallions. Serve with corn chips or sliced radishes, carrots, and celery sticks. ■

3 cups cooked black beans (page 113) or 2 (15-ounce) cans black beans, rinsed and drained

1 teaspoon chopped garlic

2 tablespoons fresh lime juice

½ cup loosely packed cilantro leaves

½ avocado, peeled

Fine sea salt

½ cup extra virgin olive oil

In a food processor, combine the beans, garlic, lime juice, cilantro, avocado, and a big pinch of salt. With the processor running, add the olive oil in a slow, steady stream until the dip is smooth. Taste and add more salt, if needed.

SUNFLOWER SEED HUMMUS MAKES 4 CUPS

This will hang out in the fridge all week long, ready for spreading on sandwiches, vegetable dipping, or—my favorite use—slathering on toasted rye bread for breakfast. Swapping a portion of chickpeas for sunflower seeds gives this hummus a nuttier flavor and airy texture. To boost the creaminess of your hummus, always use warm beans (and seeds, in this case). They're softer and break down to a velvety consistency. If you're using leftover or canned chickpeas, heat them through with their cooking liquid (or water—don't use the liquid in the can) before adding to the food processor. Mashing the minced garlic with a knife first will help it distribute evenly throughout the hummus. Serve on a piece of toasted Amanda's Bread (page 47) or with sliced raw vegetables. ∎

If setting this out as a dip for guests, sprinkle cumin, paprika, and a few sunflower seeds on top, and give it a drizzle of olive oil.

1 cup unsalted raw sunflower seeds

3 cups warm, cooked chickpeas (page 113) or 2 (15-ounce) cans chickpeas, rinsed and drained

2 tablespoons bean cooking liquid or water

1 teaspoon minced garlic, mashed with a knife

¼ cup fresh lemon juice

½ cup loosely packed flat-leaf parsley leaves

Fine sea salt

1 cup extra virgin olive oil

1 In a small saucepan, combine the sunflower seeds and 1 cup water. Bring to a boil, then remove the pan from the heat. Drain the sunflower seeds.

2 In a food processor, combine the softened sunflower seeds, chickpeas, bean liquid (or water, if using canned beans), garlic, lemon juice, parsley, and a generous pinch of salt. With the processor running, add the olive oil in a slow, steady stream until the dip is smooth. Taste and add more salt or lemon juice, if needed.

GREAT GRAINS

IN MY YEARS AS A COOK AT Gramercy Tavern in New York City, if someone told me I'd later dedicate an entire chapter of a cookbook to the virtues of whole grains, I would have laughed at the absurdity of the suggestion. Grains were in no way compelling to me—it would have seemed as likely as me writing a book on cake decorating.

But even back then, Gramercy Tavern had a strange dish on the menu with a tiny grain called amaranth. Part of what made it strange was my unfamiliarity with amaranth, which seemed like nothing more than birdseed to me. In the category of frumpy, uninspiring health food, I generally considered most whole grains to rank only marginally higher than cottage cheese. I grew up having pasta two or three nights a week, so the extent of my exposure to grains was farro (still one of my favorites) and rice, either in risotto or as a bowl of regular Carolina white rice with butter.

But building a new healthy diet meant embracing grains. They're stellar sources of fiber and complex carbohydrates, the type of carbs that take longer to digest. Getting into whole grains held practical appeal, and the cook in me was psyched because I could geek out experimenting with the massive variety out there, from the mildness of millet to nutty barley and smoky freekeh.

Now, I'm hooked. My current obsession is brown sweet rice: As it cooks, it lets out some stickiness and develops a creamy texture unlike any other brown rice I've tried. I have it along with a mountain of roasted vegetables, or I treat it like Arborio rice and make risotto out of it. Another grain I practically face-dive into is red quinoa—I find red quinoa has more structure and a nuttier taste than the white quinoa, though they're equally nutritious. Less buzzed-about but just as good is that famous amaranth, one of the grains that started my whole birdseed nonsense. I was surprised to learn that when cooked, it's similar to polenta in the way it releases a lot of starch and becomes insanely creamy. There's a decadent vibe to it.

I find grains fascinating. I love how they add texture, chew, and complexity to dishes. Every type acts and tastes differently, giving you endless options to explore in your cooking. And there are a slew of approaches to making grains exciting, if you cook them properly and throw in the right companions.

BASIC QUINOA MAKES 3 CUPS

If you have any skepticism about the appeal of grains, quinoa should be your gateway grain. Quinoa's subtle, nutty flavor and springy, chewy texture are incredibly versatile, and it cooks in 15 minutes flat. Like rice, quinoa is gluten-free, but it's more generous in the fiber department and is protein-rich, making it a go-to grain for meatless meals. White quinoa is the most common variety, but you'll find red and black too. We make a batch a couple of times a week and use it as a base for salads, toss it with leafy greens for added texture, and sprinkle it over roasted vegetables like Brussels sprouts or carrots. I especially love a few spoonfuls of quinoa stirred in a broth-based soup because it reminds me of pastina, those tiny star-shaped pastas. ∎

In its natural state, quinoa is coated in bitter-tasting compounds called saponins that are usually washed off before you buy it. Not all packaging tells you if quinoa has been prewashed, though (and you won't know if you buy quinoa from a bulk bin), so it's a good idea to give it an extra rinse.

1 cup quinoa

2 cups broth (for richer-tasting quinoa) or water

¼ teaspoon fine sea salt

1 Put the quinoa in a fine-mesh strainer and rinse it under cold water, swishing the quinoa around with your hand. Drain thoroughly.

2 In a saucepan, combine the quinoa, broth, and salt and bring to a boil over high heat. Cover, reduce the heat to low, and simmer until all the liquid is absorbed, about 15 minutes. The quinoa should look translucent and have tiny white spirals (the outer germ) around each seed.

3 Remove the pot from the heat and let it sit for 5 minutes, covered. Fluff the quinoa with a fork and serve. Store leftover quinoa in the refrigerator for up to 5 days.

QUINOA PANZANELLA SERVES 4

I grew up eating loads of panzanella every summer. While I love the classic Tuscan bread-and-tomato salad, I've found white quinoa makes a damn good version. What's cool about the quinoa here is its absorption power: Just like bread, it soaks up all the flavorful juices from the mixture of ripe tomatoes, olive oil, cucumber, basil, red onion, and capers. To make it more of a meal, my mom occasionally added a can of olive oil–poached tuna to her panzanella salad. In my version, fresh wild salmon steps in. The flavors pop a little more when this is served soon after assembly, while the salmon is still warm. But you can still expect a tasty result if you make it a couple of hours ahead of time, refrigerate it, and serve later at room temperature. If you do this, leave out the tomatoes and toss those in just before serving, so they don't make the salad soggy in the refrigerator. ∎

Don't press on or fiddle with the salmon. Fish wants to be left alone as it cooks.

Without the salmon, this salad is still delicious and filling enough for a light meal because the quinoa provides protein. It also works well as a side dish to any roasted fish.

SALMON

1 (8-ounce) skin-on wild salmon fillet

Fine sea salt and freshly ground black pepper

1 tablespoon extra virgin olive oil

SALAD

½ medium red onion, diced

½ pint cherry tomatoes, quartered

½ cucumber, quartered lengthwise and thinly sliced crosswise

½ cup fresh basil leaves, chopped

2 tablespoons capers (in brine or salt-packed), rinsed

1½ cups cooked, room temperature white quinoa (page 137)

¼ cup red wine vinegar

¼ cup extra virgin olive oil

Fine sea salt and freshly ground black pepper

1 For the salmon: Season the salmon on both sides with salt and pepper.

2 In a 10-inch skillet, heat the olive oil over high heat. As the first wisps of smoke come off the oil, add the fish to the pan skin-side down and cook for 2 minutes. Reduce the heat to medium-high and cook until the skin begins to brown, 4 to 5 minutes. Using a spatula, flip the fish and cook until it feels slightly firm when you press on it, about 2 minutes.

3 Transfer the fillet to a cutting board skin-side up. Peel off the skin and use a knife to gently scrape away the gray bloodline. With a fork, flake the fillet into little pieces.

4 For the salad: In a large bowl, combine the onion, tomatoes, cucumber, basil, and capers. Add the cooled quinoa, flaked salmon, vinegar, and olive oil and toss well. Season with salt and pepper to taste.

THE WHOLE TRUTH ABOUT WHOLE GRAINS

You know the term "whole grain" is flawed when you cruise the cereal aisle at your grocery store and see rows of boxes featuring cartoon leprechauns and toucans boasting "made with whole grains!" next to ingredient lists filled with sugars and artificial coloring. If this kind of fluff can sport a whole-grain label, how are we supposed to know what whole grains are the genuine article?

This calls for a look inside a kernel of grain. First, there's the hull—the tough and usually inedible outermost layer. Then come the integral bran and germ layers, home to flavor, fiber, protein, essential fatty acids, vitamins, and minerals. Finally, there's the starchy endosperm. When grains are refined, the nutrient-packed germ and bran are stripped away and only the endosperm is used. The refined result is the simple carbohydrate junk that I used to eat in mountainous portions: starchy, fiber-deprived foods like white flour, bagels, and white bread that have the same negative effects as eating a pile of sugar.

A whole grain contains the entire grain kernel—the bran, germ, and endosperm. But according to the U.S. Food and Drug Administration, a food can be labeled whole grain even if these three components are no longer intact. This means manufacturers can blast them apart and pulverize them before incorporating them into foods like "whole grain" cereal with rainbow marshmallows. Processing extends shelf life, but reduces grains' vitamin, fiber, and antioxidant content and raises their glycemic index (see page 35). Also, when grains are ground, the insides of the kernels are exposed to air and start to oxidize, becoming a breeding ground for free radicals. Too much exposure to free radicals and you raise the stakes on age-related disease (see page 84 for more on this).

Understanding that grain processing takes a toll doesn't mean you have to throw in the towel on them entirely. Even though they're processed, the whole wheat pastas in this chapter and the rye bread I use for breakfast sandwiches are undoubtedly more nutritionally legit and flavorful than any refined grain options. Just make sure that whole grain is listed as the first ingredient and that there are no added sugars.

For the absolute best whole-grain sources of fiber, naturally occurring vitamins, and diabetes and heart disease defense, choose *intact* whole grains. Unlike their ground-up counterparts, intact grains have gone through relatively little processing—you can still see the grain kernel—and they take longer to digest, delaying hunger and giving you lasting energy. Intact grains like quinoa, brown rice, farro, freekeh, and millet make up most of this chapter, and the steel-cut oats and buckwheat groats in the breakfast chapter fit the bill too. While it's smart to choose whole wheat bread over white bread, the real slam dunk is trading breakfast toast for a bowl of steel-cut oats and replacing a few sandwiches with grain salads.

SHAVED ASPARAGUS, AVOCADO, AND QUINOA SALAD SERVES 4

The inspiration for this salad came from my friend Jim Lahey, who has a killer pizza restaurant called Co. around the corner from where I live. They make a green salad of shaved raw asparagus and chunks of creamy avocado that lures me in as much as the pizza does. My riff on the salad has red quinoa for protein and another layer of texture, plus a handful of fresh mint, scallions, and a squeeze of lime juice. Any variety of quinoa works, but I prefer red for its deeper, nuttier flavor and the color contrast it adds. ∎

1 bunch asparagus (medium or fat stalks are best)

1 avocado, cut into ½-inch chunks

1 bunch scallions, white and pale green parts only, thinly sliced

½ cup fresh mint leaves, torn with your fingers

1½ cups cooked, room temperature red quinoa (page 137)

Juice of 1 lime

¼ cup extra virgin olive oil

Fine sea salt and freshly ground black pepper

1 Working over a cutting board, shave the asparagus into thin ribbons by holding the tough end of the spear and using a vegetable peeler to peel toward the tip. Throw away the tough ends after peeling.

2 Pile the asparagus ribbons in a large salad bowl and add the avocado, scallions, mint, and quinoa. Dress with the lime juice and olive oil and add salt and pepper to taste. Toss gently to avoid mashing up the avocado chunks.

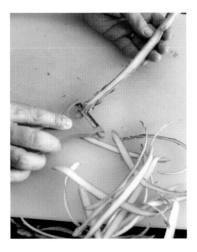

FREEKEH WITH SUGAR SNAP PEAS, SPRING ONIONS, AND FRESH HERBS SERVES 4 TO 6

I'm totally enamored with the smoky flavor of freekeh. It's a type of wheat harvested while it's still young, then sun-dried in piles, set on fire to roast, and rubbed to remove the charred husks. Freekeh's distinctive toasty, grassy notes pair best with bright flavors like the crunchy, fresh spring vegetables and fresh herbs in this salad. Though it takes longer to cook, I prefer the chewier texture of whole freekeh to the small pieces of cracked freekeh. Both varieties have double the fiber of quinoa, and more nutrients than other types of wheat. Freekeh is harder to find than other grains I use, but natural foods stores and online food retailers are safe bets. ∎

I'm always psyched to see spring onions show up at the farmers' market in May. They look like scallions with a bigger white bulb. I love the slightly sharper, brighter flavor of spring onions and use them wherever possible for the short time they're in season.

Boiling the sugar snap peas for 30 seconds takes the raw edge off while maintaining their crunch. It also brings out a more vibrant green color.

1 cup whole freekeh

Fine sea salt and freshly ground black pepper

2 cups sugar snap peas, stem ends and strings removed

4 small spring onions (or 2 bunches scallions), white and pale green parts only, thinly sliced (about ¾ cup)

5 radishes, diced

2 tablespoons chopped fresh basil leaves

2 tablespoons chopped fresh mint

2 tablespoons red wine vinegar

3 tablespoons extra virgin olive oil

1 In a pot, combine the freekeh, 5 cups water, and a couple hefty pinches of salt and bring the mixture to a boil. Reduce the heat, cover, and simmer until the grains are tender but still have some bite, about 45 minutes. Drain the freekeh, letting it sit in the colander for a few minutes to remove all the liquid. (Otherwise the dressing won't adhere to the grains.) Transfer the freekeh to a large bowl and set aside to cool.

2 Bring a pot of water to a boil. Drop in the sugar snap peas and boil until they're bright green, about 30 seconds. Strain the peas into a colander and run cold water over them. Drain the peas until they are completely dry, then cut crosswise into ¼-inch pieces.

3 Add the chopped peas, onions, radishes, basil, mint, vinegar, and olive oil to the bowl of freekeh. Toss to combine and season to taste with salt and pepper.

BASIC FARRO MAKES 5 CUPS

I may spend quality time with quinoa, sweet brown rice, and the other grains I've come to love in recent years, but farro will be in regular rotation in my kitchen forever. It's an integral wheat grain in Italian cooking, and for as long as I can remember I've loved its earthy, nutty, slightly sweet flavor. When it's cooked well, farro is tender and chewy with a bit of firmness at its center. Packing more protein and fiber than brown rice, farro makes a filling salad and adds texture and heartiness to soups (page 120). You can find it in most gourmet groceries, Italian specialty shops, and natural foods stores. ■

Farro is not gluten-free, but it has a low gluten content that people with a mild sensitivity to wheat may be able to tolerate.

2 tablespoons extra virgin olive oil

1 small yellow onion, quartered through the core

1 small carrot, quartered lengthwise

1 small celery stalk, halved lengthwise and crosswise

Fine sea salt and freshly ground black pepper

2 cups farro

1 In a large pot, heat the olive oil over medium-low heat. Add the onion, carrot, celery, and salt and pepper to taste. Stir the vegetables to thoroughly coat them with the oil. Cover, reduce the heat to low, and cook until the vegetables soften, about 10 minutes.

2 Add the farro and stir to coat it with the oil and vegetables. Add enough water to cover the farro by about ½ inch. Bring to a boil over high heat. Reduce the heat to low and simmer until the farro is tender, about 20 minutes. If the pot looks dry, add a couple tablespoons of water. Remove and discard the vegetables. Serve the farro warm, or let it cool completely before storing in the refrigerator for up to 4 days.

CRUNCHY SPRING FARRO SALAD SERVES 4 TO 6

With a premade batch of farro at the ready, this simultaneously light and substantial salad is ready in less than 10 minutes. It is exactly the way I enjoyed farro growing up—tossed with crunchy vegetables from the garden, a fresh herb, and good-quality olive oil and vinegar. Don't let its simplicity fool you—there's a great contrast of bright and earthy, cool and peppery flavors working together. This is great alongside Herb-Roasted Spatchcock Chicken (page 216). ∎

In colder months, trade the summer vegetables and basil for diced and roasted winter squash and thyme, and dress it with Honey-Cider Vinaigrette (page 58).

4 cups cooked, room temperature farro (opposite)

½ pint cherry tomatoes, halved

½ cup thinly sliced radishes

½ cucumber, quartered lengthwise and thinly sliced crosswise

1 bunch scallions, white and pale green parts only, thinly sliced

¼ cup chopped fresh basil

3 tablespoons red wine vinegar

¼ cup extra virgin olive oil

Fine sea salt and freshly ground black pepper

In a large bowl, combine the farro, tomatoes, radishes, cucumber, scallions, and basil and toss with the vinegar and olive oil. Season with salt and pepper to taste.

MUSHROOM, BARLEY, AND KALE SOUP SERVES 6 TO 8

This meat-free umami-bomb soup is immensely satisfying and full-flavored. The liquid used to rehydrate dried shiitake and porcini mushrooms creates a rich broth that's boosted by earthy, fresh cremini mushrooms and the savory depth of tomato paste and anchovies (these two melt away into the background of the soup, so you won't be able to identify them). The heady layers of umami are grounded by the nuttiness and chewy, pastalike texture of barley. Its high fiber content makes soups especially filling. It takes time to develop the deep flavors here, so this isn't a fast one. Make it over the weekend, let it cool, and then refrigerate or freeze it for quick meals during the week. ∎

Most grains have fiber only in their outer bran layer, but the fiber in barley is distributed throughout the whole kernel. So, even though the bran layer is removed from pearl barley, it still has significant amounts of fiber. You could use hulled barley here, the type that still has the bran layer, but it takes at least an hour longer to cook than pearl barley.

I'm partial to Tuscan kale, but any type of kale works well.

½ ounce dried porcini mushrooms

½ ounce dried shiitake mushrooms

¾ cup pearl barley

2 bay leaves

3 sprigs of fresh thyme tied with kitchen string, plus 1 tablespoon chopped thyme leaves

½ medium yellow onion, quartered through the core

Fine sea salt

3 tablespoons extra virgin olive oil

1 teaspoon anchovy paste (or whole anchovies chopped and mashed into a paste)

1 large carrot, cut into medium dice (about 1 cup)

1 large yellow onion, diced (about 1 cup)

4 large garlic cloves, finely chopped

1½ tablespoons tomato paste

10 ounces fresh cremini mushrooms, halved lengthwise and sliced crosswise (about 3 cups)

1 bunch kale, stems and center ribs removed, leaves chopped into bite-size pieces

Freshly grated Parmigiano-Reggiano cheese, for serving

Freshly cracked black pepper

1 In a large bowl, combine the dried porcini and shiitake mushrooms with 4 cups very hot water and let soak for 10 minutes. Squeeze the mushrooms over the bowl to release excess water, and reserve the soaking liquid. Roughly chop the porcinis and slice the shiitakes.

2 In a soup pot, combine the barley, reserved mushroom liquid, 6 cups water, the bay leaves, thyme bundle, onion, and 2 large pinches of salt. Bring to a boil, then reduce the heat to a simmer, and cook until the barley is tender but not mushy, about 20 minutes. Discard the onion quarters, thyme bundle, and bay leaves.

3 In another large soup pot, combine the olive oil, anchovy paste, carrot, onion, garlic, and a pinch of salt. Cook over high heat for 2 minutes, stirring frequently. Reduce the heat to medium, then cover, and cook the vegetables for 10 minutes, stirring once halfway through. Add the chopped thyme, tomato paste, porcinis, shiitakes, and cremini mushrooms. Stir well to combine. Cover and cook for 10 minutes, stirring once halfway through. Add the kale and another pinch of salt, stirring to coat the kale with the warm vegetables. Cover and cook for another 10 minutes, stirring occasionally.

4 Add the barley and its cooking liquid to the soup pot, along with 3 cups water. Bring the soup to a boil, then reduce the heat to a simmer, partially cover, and cook for 30 minutes. Taste and adjust the seasoning. Serve hot with Parmesan and cracked black pepper.

UMAMI

To radically enhance the flavor of your cooking without piling on salt, sugar, fat, or artificial crap, you've got to get into umami-rich foods. *Umami* is the Japanese word for "pleasant, savory taste" and is widely recognized as the fifth taste sense, joining sweet, salty, sour, and bitter. Umami adds the deep, rich, intensely savory flavor to a lot of foods you find addictively satisfying—if you've ever crumbled blue cheese over a beet salad, slurped homemade chicken soup, or simmered beans with a ham hock, you've experienced the almost indescribable deliciousness of umami. The source of its flavor-enhancing magic is an amino acid called glutamate. It exists in abundance in many foods you're already familiar with, including meat, aged cheeses, tomatoes, mushrooms, nuts, shellfish, and a few that may not be regulars in your kitchen, like miso, nori, kelp, and fish sauce.

Umami-rich ingredients are the secret to adding depth and deeply satisfying, robust flavor to meatless dishes. By packing vegetarian dishes with the powerhouse umami-rich flavors of dried and fresh mushrooms, Parmigiano-Reggiano cheese, and tomato paste, I skip the meat without sacrificing flavor. Certain cooking techniques can further amp up the flavor of umami foods: Toasting nuts and seeds, pan-roasting mushrooms, curing fish, pickling vegetables, and braising and slow-cooking all bring out a dish's inner umami, as does browning and caramelization on a well-cooked piece of meat (for a deeper dive into this, see page 198).

MUSHROOM, BARLEY,
AND KALE SOUP
(PAGE 148)

BROWN RICE RISOTTO WITH MUSHROOMS, CABBAGE, AND THYME SERVES 6 TO 8

When I had to slow down the parade of high-GI, simple carbohydrates I was eating, risotto is one of the dishes where I had to take a long, hard look. Risotto, along with pasta, is my soul food. I dedicated a big chunk of *Salt to Taste* to risotto, and there's no way it's ever coming out of my playbook. After applying the risotto technique to several whole grains, I found sweet brown rice had the best results. It has a sticky texture that gives you the same magical creaminess as Arborio rice, so you don't feel like you're settling for a second-rate version—you'll be psyched to have leftovers. ■

Other whole grains that take well to a risotto-style preparation are black rice (page 187), farro, and barley.

You could use regular green cabbage here, but I like how well the tender, crinkly ridges of savoy cabbage capture the creamy sauce of the risotto.

Risotto does not require constant stirring throughout the entire process. It's not until the moment when you're adding small increments of broth that it requires frequent stirring.

4 tablespoons extra virgin olive oil, plus more for garnish

1 (10-ounce) package cremini mushrooms, sliced (about 3 cups)

Fine sea salt and freshly ground black pepper

1 head savoy cabbage, cut into ½-inch pieces (about 3 cups)

2½ cups mushroom broth

2½ cups vegetable broth

2 tablespoons unsalted butter

1 yellow onion, diced

2 cups sweet brown rice

1 cup dry white wine

½ cup freshly grated Parmigiano-Reggiano cheese, plus more for garnish

1 tablespoon chopped fresh thyme

1 In a large high-sided skillet heat 1 tablespoon of the olive oil over high heat. Add the mushrooms and season with salt and pepper. Cook until the liquid released from the mushrooms is gone, 5 to 7 minutes. Using a silicone spatula, transfer the mushrooms to a bowl and scrape the bottom of the pan to remove and save all the flavorful bits.

2 While the pan is still hot, return it to the burner and add 1 tablespoon of the olive oil. Add the chopped cabbage and season with salt and pepper. Reduce the heat to medium-high and cook until the cabbage is wilted and slightly browned, about 10 minutes. Remove the pan from the heat.

3 Pour the mushroom and vegetable broths into a saucepan. Bring it to a boil over high heat, then reduce the heat to a simmer.

4 In a large high-sided skillet, heat 1 tablespoon of the butter and the remaining 2 tablespoons olive oil over medium heat. Add the onion and season with salt and pepper. Cook, stirring occasionally, until the onions soften, about 5 minutes.

5 Turn the heat to high and add the rice. Stir with a wooden spoon, coating the rice thoroughly with the onion, butter, and oil until the rice is crackling, 2 to 3 minutes. Add the wine. Let it bubble, stirring frequently, until the rice absorbs the wine, about 1 minute.

6 Add just enough of the warm broth to cover the rice,

about 2 cups. Reduce the heat to medium-high and stir occasionally until the rice is almost dry, about 10 minutes. Add just enough broth to cover the rice and stir every couple of minutes, until the broth is incorporated and the rice is almost dry, about 10 minutes.

7 Stirring more frequently now, continue adding warm broth to cover the rice, about ½ cup at a time, until its absorbed, every 4 to 5 minutes for 10 minutes.

8 Reduce the heat and add the cabbage, mushrooms, and about ¼ cup broth. Simmer, stirring constantly, adding ¼-cup increments of broth as needed until the rice is just tender and the risotto is a little runny (since the rice will continue to absorb moisture). Take the pan off the heat.

9 Add the Parmesan, the remaining 1 tablespoon butter, the thyme, and salt and pepper to taste, stirring to incorporate. Taste and adjust seasoning, if needed. To serve, ladle the risotto into bowls and top each serving with more freshly grated Parmesan and a drizzle of olive oil.

WHOLE WHEAT RIGATONI WITH PORCINI MUSHROOMS AND BABY SPINACH SERVES 4 TO 6

My pasta habit was a major influence in my health going off the rails. While it's still one of my biggest indulgences, I'm a more conscious eater now, so my portion size is smaller, and I occasionally swap out the simple carbs of regular white pasta for the complex carbs in whole wheat pasta. This dish is adapted from *pizzoccheri*, a Northern Italian vegetarian pasta that I make in the winter at Hearth. Readily available whole wheat pasta is an excellent substitution for the buckwheat pasta of the traditional version, and it complements the hearty flavor of mushrooms. ■

For a gluten-free pasta, try those made of a blend of quinoa and corn flours. I was surprised by how similar they are to regular semolina pasta in taste, color, and texture. Gluten-free pasta cooks quickly, so start tasting it before you think it's done.

The key step in any pasta dish is moving the pasta from its cooking water to the pan of sauce before the pasta is al dente, so it finishes cooking in the sauce. The pasta absorbs more flavor and the starch it releases helps the sauce to cling to the pasta.

1 ounce dried porcini mushrooms

¼ cup extra virgin olive oil

1 white onion, minced (about 1 cup)

3 cloves garlic, sliced paper-thin

1½ tablespoons chopped fresh thyme leaves

1½ tablespoons chopped fresh sage

3 cups baby spinach

Fine sea salt and freshly ground black pepper

1 pound whole wheat rigatoni pasta

1 tablespoon unsalted butter

3 tablespoons freshly grated Parmigiano-Reggiano cheese

¼ cup freshly shredded Fontina cheese

1 In a bowl, soak the dried porcinis in 1½ cups very hot water for 10 minutes. Strain them, reserving the soaking liquid, and finely chop them.

2 In a large high-sided skillet, combine the olive oil, onion, garlic, thyme, and sage, then turn the heat to high. Cook, stirring occasionally, until the onion is translucent, about 5 minutes. Add the chopped porcinis, spinach, and a couple pinches of salt and pepper and stir well to coat the vegetables with the oil. Reduce the heat to medium and cook for 5 minutes, stirring occasionally. Pour in the reserved porcini soaking liquid and stir. When it comes to a boil, turn off the heat.

3 Bring a large pot of salted water to a boil. Add the pasta and cook, stirring occasionally, until it's tender, but not quite al dente. Meanwhile, bring the skillet of vegetables back up to medium heat.

4 Using a spider skimmer or slotted spoon, transfer the pasta from the boiling water to the sauce in the skillet. Toss well and cook until the pasta absorbs all the liquid. If the mixture looks dry, add 2 tablespoons of the pasta cooking water. The pasta should glisten, but water shouldn't be accumulating on the bottom of the pan.

5 Add the butter and 2 tablespoons of the Parmesan and toss. If needed, add another tablespoon of pasta water. Remove the pan from the heat. To finish, sprinkle with the Fontina and the remaining 1 tablespoon Parmesan.

WHOLE WHEAT ORECCHIETTE WITH PEAS AND ONIONS SERVES 4 TO 6

You can never have too many quick-fix pantry meals in your arsenal, and this pasta proves that simple can be stellar. In a few ways, this is *cacio e pepe*, the classic Roman pasta with cheese and pepper, with the addition of peas and onions. The cheeses, good-quality butter, a generous amount of black pepper, and starchy pasta water meet up to form a creamy sauce that coats the vegetables and pasta. (As we know now, it's the refined grains in regular pasta that cause problems, not the saturated fat, so don't get anxious about the cheese and butter here!) Short pastas like orecchiette, small tubes, shells, and bow ties work best—something the peas and sauce can get lodged into. ■

2 tablespoons extra virgin olive oil

4 tablespoons unsalted butter

1 medium yellow onion, halved from root to tip and thinly sliced

2 garlic cloves, thinly sliced

Fine sea salt and freshly ground black pepper

1½ cups frozen peas, thawed

1 pound whole wheat orecchiette pasta

¼ cup freshly grated Pecorino Romano cheese, plus more for serving

¼ cup freshly grated Parmigiano-Reggiano cheese

1 In a large high-sided skillet, combine the olive oil, 2 tablespoons of the butter, the onion, and garlic. Throw in a couple of pinches of salt and pepper and cook over high heat for 3 minutes. If the onion begins to brown, bring down the heat a bit. Add the peas and toss to thoroughly coat them in the fat. Reduce the heat to medium and cook for 3 minutes. Reduce the heat to low to stew the peas and onions for 5 minutes, then turn off the heat.

2 Bring a large pot of salted water to a boil. Add the pasta and cook, stirring occasionally, until it's tender, but not quite al dente. Meanwhile, turn the heat under the peas and onions to high.

3 Using a spider skimmer or slotted spoon, lift the pasta out of the boiling water and add it to the skillet with the sauce. Add ¼ cup of the pasta water and toss. Add the Pecorino, Parmesan, the remaining 2 tablespoons butter, and a generous amount of black pepper. Add ½ cup plus 2 tablespoons more of the pasta water and salt to taste. Continue cooking, tossing frequently, until there's no liquid pooling at the bottom and the pasta has a light coating of cheese and butter. Top each serving with more freshly grated Pecorino and black pepper.

**MINT-PISTACHIO PESTO
(PAGE 161)**

ROASTED CARROTS WITH MILLET AND MINT-PISTACHIO PESTO SERVES 4

Millet draws a blank with most people even though it's been around for centuries and has an impressive nutrition profile. Yet after discovering how versatile and quick-cooking it is, I incorporate millet into a lot of dishes in my house. The small yellow grains are gluten-free and pair well with all kinds of foods. I like to amp up its slightly nutty corn flavor by toasting it before cooking. Here, the toasty cooked millet coats roasted carrots and gets a hit of minty pesto. This seems like a long time to cook carrots, but roasting them low and slow with their peel on brings out a deeper sweet flavor and a more complex, dehydrated texture. And this bright, zingy pesto is one of those things that you'll find a million uses for once you have it around. I toss it with pasta and roasted vegetables, use it as a spread on sandwiches or Chickpea Crepes (page 126), and stir a spoonful into leftover grains to give them new life. Leftover pesto can be refrigerated for up to a week, or frozen for a couple of months. ■

12 carrots, scrubbed, with tops trimmed

½ cup plus 2 tablespoons extra virgin olive oil

Fine sea salt and freshly ground black pepper

1 cup millet

1 cup loosely packed fresh mint leaves

3 tablespoons unsalted pistachios, plus chopped pistachios for serving

1 Preheat the oven to 300°F. Line a baking sheet with foil.

2 If the carrots are thicker than ½ inch, halve them lengthwise; otherwise, leave them whole. On the baking sheet, toss the carrots with 2 tablespoons of the olive oil and salt and pepper to taste. Roast, shaking the pan occasionally, until they're lightly browned and the skin looks shriveled, about 1 hour 30 minutes.

3 While the carrots roast, toast the millet in a dry pot over high heat, stirring often until the grains turn golden brown and give off a toasty fragrance, 4 to 5 minutes. Add 2¼ cups water and a pinch of salt to the pot and bring to a boil. Reduce the heat to low, cover, and simmer until most of the liquid is absorbed and the grains are fluffy, 15 to 20 minutes. Take the pot off the heat and let it sit, covered, for 10 minutes.

4 In a food processor, combine the mint, pistachios, and a pinch of salt and process until the nuts are coarsely ground. While the processor is running, add the remaining ½ cup olive oil in a slow, steady stream until the pesto is smooth.

5 On a platter or in a large bowl, toss the roasted carrots with 1 cup of the cooked millet, 3 tablespoons of the pesto, and some chopped pistachios. Season with salt and pepper to taste.

You can create a polenta-style creamy porridge using a grain-to-liquid ratio of 1:3 and stirring the millet frequently while it cooks.

If you have trouble digesting grains, give gluten-free millet a whirl. As one of the few alkaline-forming grains, it's easier to digest than most. Look for it in the bulk food section at your natural foods store. Bob's Red Mill packages it in seed form as well as in flour form, which I use to coat fried fish (page 172).

AMARANTH "POLENTA" WITH TUSCAN KALE SERVES 6 TO 8

If quinoa is the blockbuster among gluten-free grains, amaranth is the sleeper hit. When I discovered its polenta-like qualities, amaranth immediately shot up the list to become one of my favorite grains. Like cornmeal, it expands and thickens to become a luscious porridge, and amaranth brings protein power—1 cup cooked amaranth has more protein than a hard-boiled egg. You have to freeze the bunch of kale overnight, so this one takes a little planning ahead. It's much less time consuming to crumble frozen kale into tiny pieces than to mince the entire bunch. ∎

Sometimes I make this with chicken broth instead of water for a richer flavor, or I stir in a couple of tablespoons of finely chopped fresh rosemary or parsley.

1 bunch Tuscan kale (aka lacinato or dinosaur kale), frozen
Fine sea salt and freshly ground black pepper
2 cups amaranth
¼ cup freshly grated Parmigiano-Reggiano cheese
2 tablespoons extra virgin olive oil

1 Working over a bowl, crumble the frozen kale leaves with your hands until you have about 1½ cups of fine crumbles. Discard the stems and thick center ribs.

2 In a large pot, bring 6 cups water and 3 big pinches of salt to a boil over high heat. Reduce the heat to a simmer and pour the amaranth into the water in a slow, steady stream, whisking constantly. Stir in the kale and simmer, stirring occasionally, until it reaches a puddinglike consistency, about 30 minutes. The amaranth beads should be tender but retain enough shape to offer a little pop.

3 Remove the pot from the heat and stir in the Parmesan, olive oil, and a good dose of black pepper. Taste and adjust seasoning, if needed.

BULGUR WHEAT SALAD WITH ASPARAGUS, SPRING ONIONS, AND PARSLEY SERVES 4 TO 6

I like this salad to be more about the crisp freshness of asparagus than the grain, so bulgur (a form of whole wheat that's been steamed, dried, and crushed) is a great base. Its small size, light texture, and subtle, earthy flavor allow the vegetables to shine, while adding heartiness and more fiber to the salad. It also has the advantage of being one of the fastest-cooking grains. If you want more richness in the salad, toss in crumbly, dry goat cheese or ricotta salata. ∎

Spreading the bulgur in a thin layer around the sides of the bowl allows it to steam and release more moisture than if it sits in a pile in the center of the bowl. The result is drier, fluffier bulgur.

1 cup bulgur wheat

Fine sea salt and freshly ground black pepper

1 bunch asparagus

5 tablespoons extra virgin olive oil

2 medium spring onions, white and pale green parts only, thinly sliced (about 1 cup)

3 tablespoons chopped fresh parsley

2 tablespoons fresh lemon juice

1 In a pot, combine the bulgur wheat, a couple pinches of salt, and 3 cups water and bring to a boil over high heat. Reduce the heat, cover, and simmer, stirring occasionally, until the bulgur is tender but still has a little bit of a bite, 10 to 12 minutes. Thoroughly drain the excess liquid. In a large bowl, press the bulgur in a thin layer against the sides. Set aside to cool.

2 Trim the asparagus by holding each stalk horizontally and bending gently until the tough, woody end snaps off. Cut the tips from the asparagus spears and slice each tip in half lengthwise. Cut the spears crosswise into ¼-inch rounds.

3 In a large skillet, heat 2 tablespoons of the olive oil over high heat. When the first wisps of smoke come off the pan, add the asparagus tips and rounds and salt and pepper to taste. Cook for 6 minutes, tossing every couple of minutes.

4 Transfer the asparagus to the bowl with the bulgur. Add the onions, parsley, lemon juice, and remaining 3 tablespoons olive oil and toss to combine. Season with salt and pepper to taste.

FISH

LIKE MANY ITALIANS, MY FAMILY celebrates Christmas Eve with the customary Feast of the Seven Fishes. The menu changes slightly from year to year, but our multicourse seafood extravaganza covers the spectrum of seafood, from boiled calamari dressed with chile, garlic, parsley, lemon, and olive oil to lightly battered flounder pan-fried and served with lemon (a favorite I include here, page 172). And, of course, pasta—usually spaghetti or linguine with shrimp that's been sautéed with loads of parsley, garlic, and white wine. Without question, this tradition deeply rooted a love of seafood in me that continues to influence my cooking at Hearth today.

Here's the kicker: Despite how much I enjoy it, I rarely cooked seafood at home. Led by my impulses at the grocery store, I'd sooner reach for meat or poultry than fish. I suspect this is true for a lot of people, since only about one-third of Americans eat fish even once a week. Given all that fish has going for it, it's a little baffling why it ends up in the grocery cart so infrequently. Fish is a great source of lean protein and a godsend for the busy home cook; most fish cook in a matter of minutes. All but one recipe in this chapter call for under 30 minutes of active cooking time—most are closer to 15 minutes.

Fish also offer unbeatable health benefits, namely their content of omega-3 fatty acids (page 174).

Maybe it's because people find cooking fish too challenging to mess with at home. This perception couldn't be further from the truth. Fish is generally easier to cook than meat; it's simply a matter of becoming comfortable with a few basic techniques. Roasting and grilling may be the two most popular methods, but if you're a fish-wary cook, I suggest starting with steaming and poaching. The gentle heat and moisture involved in the duo of poached fish and clam recipes (pages 184 and 185) and Steamed Black Bass with Bok Choy (page 189) reduce the likelihood of overcooking, so the result is succulent, flavor-infused fish. Another foolproof way to protect delicate fish from drying out is to bake it in parchment paper, which holds in moisture and concentrates the flavor of the Wild Salmon in Parchment with Olives, Fennel, and Lemon (opposite).

Regardless of technique, choosing high-quality fish and cooking it the day you buy it is paramount. The taste and texture of freshly caught local fish is always going to be superior to days-old (or older) frozen fish from a different continent. And while there's not a universal answer to the question of wild or farmed, the better option is usually wild fish caught using sustainable methods (like hook and line fishing). The discussion of factory-farmed beef and poultry is now mainstream (page 200), but there's relatively little awareness about the practices at average fish farms. Penned in close quarters, fed an artificial diet, and treated with antibiotics and dyes, most farmed fish, especially farmed Atlantic salmon, are damaging to the surrounding ecosystems and have less omega-3s and protein than wild fish. All farmed fish are not created equal, so the best thing to do is tap into the knowledge of your local market's fishmonger. Ask if the fish is local or shipped in, wild-caught, or farmed. You can also refer to the Monterey Bay Aquarium's Seafood Watch (seafoodwatch.org) as a guide.

Among the most sustainable sources wild fish are oily, delicious little fish like sardines and anchovies. I'm a crusader for these little guys not only because they're inexpensive and widely available, but because they're full of umami-rich flavor (see page 149) and complexity. They're also low on the food chain, so they don't contain toxins found in other types of seafood. My other fish obsession was confirmed with my recent purchase of an entire side of wild Alaskan salmon. I cut it into 6-ounce portions, which now fill our freezer at home. Pan-roasted, cured, poached, or baked, the buttery texture and richness of salmon is king for me lately.

WILD SALMON IN PARCHMENT WITH OLIVES, FENNEL, AND LEMON SERVES 4

Cooking in parchment paper (or foil) packets is a quick, low-effort way to get juicy, delicious fish every time. Even though you can't see or touch the fish, you can trust it'll turn out great. The sealed packet locks moisture in, so the fish steams perfectly along with any flavorings you add. I like the classic combo of fennel and lemon with the addition of a few briny olives, but don't feel boxed in by this suggestion—whatever floats your boat will work. Keep in mind that everything in the packet has 12 minutes to cook, so be sure to thinly slice your raw vegetables. You can make this for one and cook it in a toaster oven, or easily scale this up to create packets for a larger group. You'll feel like a champ as everyone eagerly tears open their individual packet and "ooohs" and "ahhs" as the steam puffs out. ■

4 teaspoons extra virgin olive oil, plus 3 tablespoons for drizzling

16 thin lemon slices (about 2 lemons)

Fine sea salt and freshly ground black pepper

4 (6- to 8-ounce) skinless wild salmon fillets

1 large fennel bulb, thinly sliced

20 olives, pitted and roughly chopped (I like using assorted olives—any variety works)

2 teaspoons fresh thyme leaves

1 Preheat the oven to 400°F. Fold 4 large pieces of parchment paper in half, then cut a half oval in each piece of folded paper, so you get rounded cutouts that are folded in the middle like a clamshell.

2 Unfold the parchment and brush 1 teaspoon of olive oil in the center of one half of each paper. Lay 3 lemon slices side by side on the oiled area of each one, sprinkle with salt and pepper, and top with a salmon fillet. Place the remaining slice of lemon on top of each fish, then the fennel slices and olives on top of each. Scatter the thyme

leaves and drizzle the remaining 3 tablespoons olive oil over all. Add a generous pinch of salt to each packet.

3 To seal, fold the other half of parchment over the fish, so the two edges line up. Working from one side to the other, fold the edges over an inch or so and tightly crimp them closed.

4 Put the packets on a baking sheet and steam the fish in the oven for 12 minutes. Remove from the oven and transfer each parchment package to a plate.

WILD SALMON IN PARCHMENT
WITH OLIVES, FENNEL, AND LEMON
(PAGE 169)

PASSERA FRITA (PAN-FRIED FLOUNDER) SERVES 4

A ridiculously simple and tasty fried flounder is one of my favorite things we do in our evening-long parade of fish dishes on Christmas Eve. Because it's not deep-fried in copious amounts of vegetable oil, beer-battered, or smothered in tartar sauce, it's a fried fish that I have no problem digging into. The flounder takes a dip in flour, then beaten egg, and gets pan-fried in olive oil. After a squeeze of lemon juice and a sprinkle of parsley, it's outrageously good. I now trade all-purpose white flour for whole-grain millet flour with no love lost—it has more fiber and protein, and is gluten-free. Millet flour also gives you a nice crispy coating, and its yellow hue enhances the golden brown exterior. ∎

4 (4- to 5-ounce) skinless flounder fillets

Fine sea salt and freshly ground black pepper

¼ cup millet flour

2 large eggs

2 tablespoons whole milk

4 tablespoons extra virgin olive oil

1 lemon, cut into wedges

2 teaspoons chopped fresh flat-leaf parsley

1 Lightly season the fish on both sides with salt and pepper. Pour the millet flour onto a plate. Beat the eggs with the milk in a wide shallow bowl and season with salt and pepper.

2 Heat 2 tablespoons of olive oil in a skillet over high heat. Working in batches, dredge the fish in the flour, then shake off the excess and dip the fillets into the egg. Add two coated fillets to the pan and cook until golden brown on the bottom, 1 to 2 minutes. Turn each fillet and cook until the second side is golden and crispy, about 1 minute more. Transfer the fish to a plate. Add the remaining 2 tablespoons olive oil to the pan and repeat the dredging and frying process with the 2 remaining fillets.

3 Serve the fish with the lemon wedges and chopped parsley.

OMEGA-3 FATTY ACIDS

The Anti-Inflammatory Superstars

There's usually some truth to old-school wisdom, and the one about fish as "brain food" is no exception. It has to do with omega-3 fatty acids, the healthy fat found in abundance in certain kinds of cold-water fish and, to a lesser degree, foods like flaxseeds and grass-fed meats. Assuming you've embraced the fact that not all fat is dangerous for your heart and the size of your belly (page 22), you know that healthy eating isn't about cutting out fat, but rather adding in the good fats. Among these, omega-3 fatty acids have become the MVP. Even if you've only half-heartedly glanced at nutritional recommendations, you've likely heard about them because experts of every approach to healthy eating—from grain-free and low-carb diets to vegetarian and vegan—agree that omega-3s are undeniably good for you.

Rattling off the list of their health benefits sounds a little like a late-night infomercial. If you consistently get enough omega-3s, over time you could have better memory, brighter moods, protection against the symptoms of depression, improved asthma, and good skin, hair, and eyesight. Remembering where you put your keys and being able to read the menu in a dark restaurant may be reason enough to make sure you're getting your omega-3s, but it's their anti-inflammatory powers that make them a critical nutrient. Inflammation in the body is normal when it's in response to an injury like a sprained ankle or cut on your finger, but chronic inflammation caused by years of too much stress and a shitty diet of processed food can kill ya. You can't see this type of inflammation, but it's the driving force behind most diseases, ranging from cancer and heart disease to Alzheimer's, Crohn's, and arthritis.

Omega-3s are an essential fat for human health, but our bodies can't produce them—we have to get them from food. The main types of omega-3s are ALA, EPA, and DHA. ALAs are in plant foods like chia seeds, flaxseeds, walnuts, and all cooking oils made from vegetables, nuts, or seeds. The more potent and most beneficial types of omega-3s are EPA and DHA, found in fatty cold-water fish, including salmon, anchovies, sardines, mackerel, herring, and tuna. Both EPA and DHA can help lower blood pressure, slow the rate of gunk build-up in arteries, and increase good cholesterol. EPA in particular works as an anti-inflammatory in the brain where its help with blood flow may fight depression and prevent Alzheimer's (brain food!).

You can't talk about omega-3s without considering their close cousins, omega-6s—you need both types of fat so your body hums along like it should. Omega-6s are pro-inflammatory, but this isn't a big deal if you're getting enough omega-3 fats to balance them. The problem comes in when you rarely eat omega-3–rich foods and overload on omega-6s in the form of cheap, grain-fed meats and highly processed vegetable oils like soybean, corn, and sunflower oils (hydrogenating these oils turns them into trans fat—another damaging fat that provokes inflammation). When the balance of these fats

is out of whack, the omega-6s crowd out the omega-3s and cause chronic inflammation. The recommended ratio of omega-6 to omega-3 is 2:1; these days, the typical American has an out-of-control ratio somewhere between 10:1 and 20:1, mostly because of the glut of vegetable oils in processed food.

When I was diagnosed with gout, a form of arthritis, I shifted my diet to focus on foods packed with omega-3s (along with alkaline-forming foods, page 56). The more omega-3 fat I ate, the less omega-6 was available to stir up inflammation in my joints. Extra virgin olive oil has always been my go-to cooking oil, but all the processed food I ate—the bags of chips, late-night burgers, and deli meats—are

omega-6 bombs. To fix the imbalance, I started eating omega-3–rich fish a couple times a week, specifically salmon, anchovies, and sardines. When I buy meat, eggs, and butter, I seek out grass-fed and pasture-raised options, which are much higher in omega-3 fatty acids. I also work in chia seeds, flaxseeds, and walnuts. Omega-3 supplements can be a kind of insurance, but, as always, I prefer to get nutrients from my diet first. Plus, choking down fish oil isn't nearly as enjoyable as eating silky Cured Salmon (page 177), Whole Wheat Spaghetti "Con Sarde" (page 192), Grass-Fed Beef Meatloaf (page 220), or Pecan Power Balls (page 243). Eating omega-3–rich foods is probably the most delicious nutrition recommendation out there.

CURED SALMON SERVES 4 TO 6

I'm a huge fan of the silky-smooth, sliceable flesh of cured salmon, and surprisingly little is required to make it at home: a quality piece of fish, herb-and-citrus-spiked salt, and a little patience for the 24 hours it takes to cure. A major advantage of curing is that it removes moisture from the fish, thereby preserving it and allowing you to eat from it all week. Slice it up to have with eggs, pile it on toasted bread with capers and red onion, or have a few shavings as a snack. You can also set out a big hunk of it as a party appetizer or for breakfast when you have company. Ask the person at the fish counter for the top, thick end of the salmon, not the tail end; using a thicker cut of fish with more flesh gives you a tastier result. ■

Once you've got the method down, you can customize the cure to include your favorite herbs and spices. To name a few—dill, fennel seeds, ground coriander, and orange or grapefruit zest would all be great here.

1 cup fine sea salt

2 tablespoons coarsely ground black pepper

Finely grated zest of 2 lemons

2 tablespoons chopped fresh rosemary

2 tablespoons chopped fresh sage

2 tablespoons chopped fresh thyme

1 pound wild skin-on salmon fillet (about 6 inches long and 1½ inches thick)

1 In a bowl, combine the salt, pepper, lemon zest, and herbs.

2 Pat the salmon dry on both sides with a paper towel and lay it skin-side up on a cutting board. With a sharp knife, score the skin diagonally in 3 places, being careful not to slice into the flesh. (This allows the salmon flesh to draw in the salt and cure faster.)

3 Put several long pieces of plastic wrap over a baking sheet. In the center, arrange half the salt mixture in a mound the same length as the salmon fillet. Place the fish skin-side down over the mound, then spread the remaining salt mixture evenly over the flesh side of the salmon. Wrap the salmon tightly in the plastic wrap. Put another baking sheet on top and weight it with several heavy jars or cans, sandwiching the wrapped salmon in between the pans. Refrigerate for 24 hours. After this time, the salmon flesh should feel firm, but not hard. (If it's squishy, wrap it back up and refrigerate for another day.)

4 Unwrap the salmon and rinse off the cure under cold water. Pat it dry with paper towels. Use a sharp, nonserrated knife to slice the flesh into paper-thin pieces. Store in the refrigerator for up to a week.

SALMON AND ARUGULA SALAD WITH POMEGRANATE SERVES 4

This is one of my go-to meals when I'm taking it easy on high-carbohydrate foods. Especially when I'm at the restaurant, where bread and pasta are staring me in the face all day, I need a super simple lunch that's fast, filling, and jammed with flavor. This salad is everything I want. There are a few ways to dress it—as with most salads, I'm a big fan of the on-the-fly method—just a squeeze of lemon, drizzle of olive oil, salt, and pepper. Of course, you could also make a vinaigrette, such as my Lemon Vinaigrette with Garlic and Anchovy (page 61) and use that here. ■

Two important points for sautéing and pan-roasting fish: (1) make sure your pan is very hot and (2) once you add the fish to the pan, leave it alone! The fish will develop a nice crust and release perfectly when you go to flip the pieces.

10 ounces arugula

2 (8-ounce) skinless wild salmon fillets

Fine sea salt and freshly ground black pepper

5 tablespoons extra virgin olive oil

1 cup pomegranate seeds

2 tablespoons fresh lemon juice

1 small red onion, thinly sliced

1 Add the arugula to a large salad bowl. Season the fish on both sides with salt and pepper and cut each fillet into 5 even slices.

2 In a large skillet, heat 2 tablespoons of the olive oil over high heat. When the oil slides easily across the pan and wisps of smoke come off the surface, add the salmon and cook, untouched, for 2 minutes. Flip the pieces and cook for 30 seconds on the other side.

3 Put the hot salmon pieces on top of the greens, cover the bowl with a plate or baking sheet, and set aside for 5 minutes to wilt the arugula.

4 Drop the pomegranate seeds into the bowl, along with the remaining 3 tablespoons olive oil, salt to taste, a good dose of black pepper, the lemon juice, and red onion. Using a fork, lightly break up the pieces of salmon into large flakes. Toss well to combine.

SHRIMP AND CHICKPEA TRIFOLATI SERVES 4 TO 6

Trifolati refers to the classic Italian method of sautéing with garlic, parsley, and olive oil. My love for the flavor-packed simplicity of trifolati runs deep. There's a version with mushrooms in *Salt to Taste*, but I love it applied to shrimp and chickpeas for a fast, protein-loaded meal. You can get a ton of mileage out of this recipe: It works great with onions, carrots, cauliflower, zucchini, scallops, and thin pieces of beef or chicken. The key to trifolati is finely chopping the parsley, garlic, and lemon zest together on the cutting board until they become one. The resulting mixture is so much greater than the sum of its parts. ■

There are a few variations on the basic trifolati mixture that are worth trying. In step 2, try adding red pepper flakes or minced peperoncini along with the parsley and garlic.

1 pound (21/25) shrimp, peeled and deveined (leave the tails on)

1 cup loosely packed fresh flat-leaf parsley leaves

2 large garlic cloves

Finely grated zest and juice of 1 lemon, plus a squeeze more for serving

3 tablespoons extra virgin olive oil, plus more for serving

2 cups cooked chickpeas (page 113) or 1 (15-ounce) can chickpeas, rinsed and drained

1 Rinse the shrimp and pat dry with paper towels.

2 Ball the parsley in your fist and press it onto a cutting board. Run your knife several times through the ball to roughly chop the leaves. Cut the garlic cloves in half across the equator, smash each half with the flat side of your knife, and roughly chop them. Put the garlic and lemon zest on top of the pile of parsley and finely chop them together. The mixture should yield about ½ cup of trifolati.

3 In a large skillet, heat the olive oil over high heat. Once wisps of smoke come off the pan, add the shrimp in a single layer. Season with salt and pepper, and cook without touching the shrimp for 2 minutes. Add the trifolati and toss to coat the shrimp. Add the chickpeas and lemon juice and toss to combine. Season with salt and pepper to taste. Cook for 3 minutes more, allowing the flavors to combine and everything to become evenly coated with the trifolati. Pour into a serving bowl and top with a squeeze of lemon juice and a drizzle of olive oil.

HALIBUT LIVORNESE SERVES 4

For Italian seafood inspiration, I often look to the city of Livorno on the Tuscan coast where fish dishes prepared *alla Livornese* contain tomatoes, olives, and capers. One of the most delicious and easiest of these preparations is made with fresh white fish—usually whatever the catch of the day is. Baking the fish while embedded in the rich sauce infuses it with flavor and keeps it moist. Any fresh, firm-fleshed white fish takes well to this approach, including striped bass, monkfish, tilapia, and cod. Keep in mind that the baking time may vary depending on the type and thickness of fish you use. ∎

4 tablespoons extra virgin olive oil

⅓ cup minced yellow onion

⅓ cup minced fennel

2 garlic cloves, thinly sliced

3 tablespoons chopped fresh basil

Fine sea salt and freshly ground black pepper

1 (28-ounce) can whole peeled tomatoes, drained and chopped

⅓ cup pitted black olives (I like Taggiasca or niçoise)

2 tablespoons capers, rinsed

4 (5- to 6-ounce) halibut fillets

1 Preheat the oven to 350°F.

2 In a large ovenproof skillet combine the olive oil, onion, fennel, garlic, 1 tablespoon of the basil, and a pinch of salt, then turn the heat to medium-high. Cook for 5 minutes, reduce the heat to medium, and cook, stirring occasionally, until the vegetables have softened and become translucent, about 3 minutes.

3 Add the tomatoes, olives, and capers and increase the heat to high. Season with salt and pepper to taste. (The olives and capers add a good amount of salt, so start with a little and taste as you go.) Cook for 3 minutes, breaking up the tomatoes with a wooden spoon. Reduce the heat to medium-high and continue to lightly cook until the sauce has slightly thickened, about 5 minutes.

4 Stir in the remaining 2 tablespoons basil. Lightly season the halibut fillets on both sides with salt and pepper. Nestle them into the sauce, spooning some sauce over the top of each one until they're mostly submerged. After 1 minute, transfer the pan to the oven and bake until the fish flakes apart with a fork or gives easily when lightly squeezed, about 10 minutes. Plate the fillets and spoon the sauce over each one.

POACHED BLACK BASS AND CLAMS WITH SPRING VEGETABLES AND MINT SERVES 4

In this low-hassle, single-pan meal, black bass fillets gently cook in a shallow pool of clam-and-wine-infused broth that's so aromatic, you're compelled to stick your face in the bowl, eyes closed, and breathe it in. Asparagus, scallions, and three kinds of peas bring crunch and vibrant freshness, and ginger adds a subtle kick. Even though poaching gives you more leeway than roasting or grilling, you can still overcook the fish if the poaching liquid is boiling, so keep it at a low simmer for gentle cooking. ∎

1 bunch asparagus

4 (6-ounce) skin-on black sea bass fillets

1 dozen littleneck clams

3 tablespoons extra virgin olive oil, plus more for serving

1 garlic clove, thinly sliced

½-inch piece fresh ginger, peeled and thinly sliced

1 bunch scallions, white and pale green parts only, thinly sliced

½ cup halved snow peas, stem ends and strings removed

½ cup halved sugar snap peas, stem ends and strings removed

½ cup frozen peas

Fine sea salt and freshly ground black pepper

½ cup dry white wine

3 tablespoons white wine vinegar

¼ cup torn fresh mint leaves

1 Trim the asparagus by snipping off the tough, woody ends.

2 With a sharp knife, score the skin of each fillet, making three diagonal slashes about 1 inch apart. Scrub any sand and grit off the clams, then soak them in a bowl of cold water for 20 minutes.

3 In a large, shallow pan, combine the olive oil, garlic, ginger, and scallions, then turn the heat to high. Once the oil sizzles, add the asparagus, snow peas, sugar snaps, frozen peas, and a big pinch of salt and stir to coat with the oil. Reduce the heat to medium, cover, and cook, stirring every 3 minutes, until the vegetables are soft, but not browned, about 9 minutes.

4 Drain and rinse the clams and add them to the pan. Add the wine, vinegar, and ¼ cup water. Cover, increase the heat to medium-high, and cook until the clams open, about 5 minutes. Reduce the heat to low.

5 Lightly season both sides of the fillets with salt and pepper and nestle them in a single layer among the vegetables and clams. The liquid should be just below an active simmer. Cover and poach the fish for 5 minutes. The fish is done when it's opaque and tender when you pierce in the thickest part. Stir in the mint leaves and taste the broth, adding salt or pepper, if needed.

6 To serve, place a fillet and 3 clams in each bowl and ladle the vegetables and broth over.

POACHED RED SNAPPER AND CLAMS WITH WINTER VEGETABLES SERVES 4

When you eat with the seasons, using ingredients when they're at their best, food simply tastes better. It's instinctual to be drawn to heartier flavors in the winter and lighter flavors in the warm months—it just feels right. But this doesn't mean you have to say goodbye to some of your favorite dishes for half the year. In this case, I've winterized a spring dish that I love by using hearty vegetables that are in season in the colder months. While the technique is basically the same, you get a completely different flavor that's more in line with a cold night by the fire. This version of poached fish and clams has a curative effect, in the way that chicken soup does. When I need a rest from heavier stews and meaty braises, I turn to this. ∎

4 (6-ounce) skin-on red snapper fillets

1 dozen littleneck clams

3 tablespoons extra virgin olive oil, plus more for serving

1 medium carrot, thinly sliced

1 small celery stalk, thinly sliced

1 small fennel bulb, thinly sliced

½ leek, white and pale green parts only, halved lengthwise and sliced crosswise, washed

½ small white onion, sliced

2 small garlic cloves, sliced

1 bay leaf

1 sprig of fresh rosemary

Fine sea salt and freshly ground black pepper

½ cup dry white wine

3 tablespoons white wine vinegar

¼ cup chopped fresh flat-leaf parsley

1 With a sharp knife, score the skin of each fillet, making three diagonal slashes about 1 inch apart. Scrub any sand and grit off the clams, then soak them in a bowl of cold water for 20 minutes.

2 In a large shallow pan, heat the olive oil over high heat. Once the oil starts to shimmer, add the carrot, celery, fennel, leek, onion, garlic, bay leaf, rosemary, and a big pinch of salt and stir to coat with the oil. Reduce the heat to medium, cover, and cook, stirring every 3 minutes, until the vegetables are soft, but not browned, about 9 minutes.

3 Drain and rinse the clams and add them to the pan. Add the wine, vinegar, and ¼ cup water. Cover, nudge the heat up to medium-high, and cook until the clams open, about 5 minutes. Reduce the heat to low.

4 Lightly season both sides of the fillets with salt and pepper and nestle them in a single layer among the vegetables and clams. The liquid should have the tiniest amount of movement— not an active simmer. Cover and poach the fish for 5 minutes. The fish is done when it's opaque and there's little resistance when you insert a knife in the thickest part. Taste the broth and adjust the seasoning with salt and pepper if needed.

5 Place a fillet and 3 clams in each bowl and ladle the vegetables and broth over each. Serve with a drizzle of olive oil and the parsley.

BLACK RICE SEAFOOD RISOTTO SERVES 4 TO 6

This exotic risotto tastes as impressive as it looks, earning you Hosting Hall of Fame status with any guests at your dinner table. It balances the deep, nutty richness of black rice with the tender sweetness of calamari and shrimp and noticeable heat from the peperoncini. The seafood cooks in about 2 minutes, so the majority of your effort is focused on the black rice. Also called forbidden rice, black rice is a trip: Once cooked, it turns dark purple, and the kernels are very chewy, retaining a slight bite even after they're fully cooked (unlike the creamier Arborio rice). It's insanely delicious. ■

Black rice has all the benefits of brown rice, with the added perk of some serious anthocyanin antioxidants, the same ones that give blueberries and blackberries their deep, inky color. The hard outer shell of black rice holds all this goodness, but also makes its cooking time longer than white rice, and even a bit longer than brown rice.

Sometimes I boil the water in a teapot, making it easier to pour each addition of water into the pan of rice.

Finely grated zest of 2 lemons

1 bunch fresh flat-leaf parsley, chopped (about 1 cup)

3 tablespoons extra virgin olive oil

3 dried peperoncini (or ¼ teaspoon red pepper flakes), minced

1 medium yellow onion, minced (about 1½ cups)

5 garlic cloves, minced (about 1 tablespoon)

2 cups black rice (like Lundberg Black Japonica or Forbidden Rice)

Fine sea salt

¾ cup dry white wine

1 pound cleaned squid rinsed in cool water and cut into thin rings (about ⅛ inch thick), large tentacles halved

½ pound (21/25) shrimp, peeled, deveined, and chopped into small pieces

1 cup halved grape tomatoes

2 tablespoons fresh lemon juice

1 In a pot (or kettle), bring 10 cups of water to a boil, then reduce the heat to a simmer.

2 Pile the lemon zest on top of the chopped parsley and finely chop them together.

3 In a large high-sided skillet, heat the olive oil over high heat. When the oil is hot and slides easily across the pan, add the peperoncini, onion, and garlic, stirring to coat with the oil. Fry for 1 minute, then reduce the heat to medium-high and cook, stirring occasionally, until the onions are translucent, about 5 minutes. Add the rice and a pinch of salt, stirring to coat the rice with the oil and onions. Toast the rice for 3 minutes, stirring frequently.

RECIPE CONTINUES

4 Add the wine. Let it bubble, stirring occasionally, until it's absorbed, about 3 minutes. Add just enough hot water to cover the rice, about 2 cups, and cook, stirring and scraping rice away from the sides occasionally until the liquid is mostly absorbed, about 12 minutes. Again, add just enough hot water to cover the rice and stir every couple of minutes, until the broth is incorporated and the rice is almost dry, 10 to 12 minutes. Continue adding hot water just to cover the rice, stirring occasionally and waiting until the water is absorbed to add more, about 30 minutes.

5 Stirring more frequently now, continue adding the remaining hot water to cover the rice, about ½ cup at a time, until it's absorbed, about every 5 minutes, for 10 to 15 minutes. When it's fully cooked, the rice will be firm, but tender and somewhat chewy.

6 Add the squid, shrimp, tomatoes, and a big pinch of salt. Cook for 2 minutes, stirring frequently. Remove the pan from the heat and add the lemon-parsley mixture and the lemon juice. Taste and adjust the seasoning with salt. If the rice has started to go dry and sticky (it continues to absorb water even off the heat), add a little more water to loosen it before serving.

STEAMED BLACK BASS WITH BOK CHOY SERVES 4

There's no better way to bring out the clean, pure flavors of fresh fish than by steaming it. In a simple, two-tiered Chinese bamboo steamer, the fish is surrounded with moist heat, so there's little danger of it drying out, and you can subtly infuse it with any herbs, citrus, or seasonings you like. There's not a lot to this process, so seeking the best-quality, freshest fish is especially important. I like the mild sweetness of black sea bass, but any firm-fleshed white fish, including halibut and red snapper, will work just as well. Serve this with a bowl of steamed sweet brown rice. ∎

4 (5- to 6-ounce) skin-on black bass fillets

2 heads bok choy, halved through the core

Fine sea salt and freshly ground black pepper

6 teaspoons extra virgin olive oil

2 lemons, sliced

1-inch piece fresh ginger, peeled and thinly sliced

Soy-Ginger Vinaigrette (page 59), to taste

1 Season the fillets and the bok choy on both sides with salt and pepper. Brush each fillet with 1 teaspoon of the olive oil and toss the bok choy with the remaining 2 teaspoons olive oil.

2 Pour 3 inches of water into a pot. Make sure the bamboo steamer can sit on top of the pot with about 1 inch of space between the water and the bottom of the steamer. Bring the water to a boil over high heat, then reduce to a simmer.

3 Line the bottom of two steamer baskets with the lemon slices and evenly distribute the ginger on top of the lemon. In each basket, arrange 2 fillets skin-side up and 2 halves of bok choy in a single layer. Stack the baskets and cover with the bamboo top. Place the entire steamer basket on top of the pot of simmering water and steam until the bok choy is tender, the fish is opaque, and a thin knife poked in a seam in the flesh meets little resistance, 5 to 7 minutes.

4 Season the fish and bok choy with a sprinkle of salt and add Soy-Ginger Vinaigrette.

SALMON TACOS WITH GUACAMOLE, SALSA, AND CABBAGE-RADISH SLAW SERVES 4 TO 6

Everybody's happy with fish tacos. Something about this meal feels celebratory, even if it's a random Monday night. At least once a year I make fish tacos with my family on Martha's Vineyard, using fresh local striped bass. It's perfect summertime eating—clean, fresh Mexican flavors, rather than the heavy fried stuff. At home, I usually use salmon, but you can substitute any firm white fish. ∎

12 corn tortillas

2 tablespoons extra virgin olive oil

1¼ pounds skinless wild salmon fillet, cut into 12 pieces

Fine sea salt and freshly ground black pepper

Tomato Salsa (recipe follows)

Guacamole (recipe follows)

Cabbage-Radish Slaw (recipe follows)

Sour cream, sliced jalapeños, and lime wedges, for serving

1 Preheat the oven to 200°F. Line the bottom of a baking pan with a damp paper towel and add a stack of tortillas. Cover with another damp paper towel and seal the pan with foil. Warm in the oven while the fish cooks.

2 In a large skillet, heat the olive oil over high heat. Season the salmon pieces on both sides with salt and pepper. When you see wisps of smoke coming off the pan, add the salmon and sear for 1½ minutes on both sides.

3 Fill the warmed tortillas with salmon and top with salsa, guacamole, and slaw. Garnish with sour cream, jalapeños, and a squeeze of fresh lime.

TOMATO SALSA
MAKES ABOUT 3 CUPS

I like a mild salsa that highlights the freshness of tomatoes, but you can fire it up with the addition of finely chopped jalapeño and serrano peppers. This salsa depends entirely on having good-quality tomatoes—don't even attempt this with mealy or blah, out-of-season ones.

3 tomatoes, diced (about 2 cups)

1 bunch scallions, thinly sliced (about ½ cup)

2 tablespoons chopped fresh cilantro

2 tablespoons extra virgin olive oil

Juice of 1 lime

Fine sea salt and freshly ground black pepper

In a bowl, combine the tomatoes, scallions, cilantro, olive oil, lime juice, and salt and pepper to taste. Stir to combine.

GUACAMOLE
MAKES ABOUT 2 CUPS

Avocados may be the closest you can get to a perfect food. They have good monounsaturated fat, fiber, and antioxidants, but what drives my uncontrollable obsession is their creamy, luscious texture. I'm always looking for new ways to eat avocados, but guacamole never gets old. If your avocados are slightly under-ripe, chop them and add to a bowl with the lime juice and a sprinkle of salt to soften up for 5 minutes before adding the rest of the ingredients.

2 avocados, roughly chopped

½ cup quartered grape tomatoes

½ red onion, diced (about ½ cup)

1 small fresh jalapeño pepper, seeded, ribbed, and minced (about 1½ teaspoons)

2 tablespoons chopped fresh cilantro

2 tablespoons extra virgin olive oil

Juice of 1 lime

Fine sea salt and freshly ground black pepper

In a large bowl, combine the avocados, tomatoes, onion, jalapeño, cilantro, olive oil, lime juice, and salt and black pepper to taste. Toss the ingredients together and roughly mash the avocado with a fork until you reach the level of smoothness you like.

CABBAGE-RADISH SLAW
MAKES ABOUT 3½ CUPS

I keep the slaw bright and tangy, so it's a crunchy, light counterpoint to the richness of the salmon and guacamole, and the olive oil in the salsa.

3 cups shredded green cabbage (about 1 medium head)

3 radishes, thinly sliced

2 tablespoons chopped fresh cilantro

Juice of 2 limes

1½ teaspoons fine sea salt

In a large bowl, toss together the cabbage, radishes, cilantro, lime juice, and salt. Let the slaw marinate for 15 minutes.

WHOLE WHEAT SPAGHETTI "CON SARDE" SERVES 4 TO 6

The briny, salty flavor of sardines plays a big role in a lot of Mediterranean and Italian dishes, but it's this classic Sicilian pasta that I go back to again and again. Primarily made with inexpensive pantry staples, there is a perfect balance of textures and flavors in this dish. The intensity of sardines mellows out in a sauce of fennel, raisins, olive oil, and the salty umami of anchovies, and the whole thing gets a shower of toasted pine nuts and fennel fronds for a satisfying crunch. If you've previously shied away from sardines, this is a great place to start bringing out the best of these little beauties. ■

Sardines are high in omega-3s and contain almost no mercury. They're usually found in canned form, but if you have the good fortune of finding fresh, plump sardines, a pound of those would be outstanding here. Ask your fishmonger to remove the heads, tails, and backbones.

Don't drain the pasta in a colander—the starchy pasta water is used to moisten the pasta once it goes into the pan with the sauce.

¼ cup golden raisins

¼ cup toasted pine nuts

½ fennel bulb, minced, fronds reserved

2 olive oil–packed anchovy fillets

1 large garlic clove

1 pound whole wheat spaghetti

6 tablespoons extra virgin olive oil

½ white onion, minced

Fine sea salt and freshly ground black pepper

1 teaspoon tomato paste

2 (4-ounce) tins olive oil–packed sardines, drained and rinsed

¼ cup chopped fresh flat-leaf parsley

Juice of ½ lemon

1 Place the raisins in a small bowl and add just enough warm water to cover. Set aside to soak for at least 10 minutes.

2 Finely chop the pine nuts and fennel fronds together and set aside (see page 195). Mince the anchovy fillets and garlic together, then mash them into a paste (see page 61).

3 Bring a large pot of salted water to a boil over high heat. Add the pasta and cook, stirring occasionally, until it's tender, but not quite al dente, 1 to 2 minutes less than the package says.

4 While the pasta cooks, in a large skillet, combine 4 tablespoons of the olive oil, the minced fennel bulb, onion, and a pinch of salt over high heat. Cook until the vegetables begin to soften, about 5 minutes. Stir in the garlic-anchovy paste and cook for 1 minute. Add the tomato paste and stir to coat the vegetables. Cook for 1 minute, then add 3 tablespoons water and toss. Drain the raisins and add them to the pan along with the sardines and a pinch of salt. Cook for 2 minutes more. If waiting on your pasta, turn the heat off until just before you're ready to add the cooked pasta.

5 When the pasta is ready, use tongs to lift it out of the water and into the pan. Add ¼ cup of the pasta water and the parsley to the pan and cook, tossing frequently, for about 3 minutes. If needed, add another little bit of pasta water so the pasta is just wet. Add the lemon juice, the remaining 2 tablespoons olive oil, and salt and pepper to taste and toss well. Plate the pasta and sprinkle generously with the pine nut and fennel frond mixture.

TOASTED PINE NUTS
AND FENNEL FRONDS (PAGE 192)

MEAT & POULTRY

WHEN YOU CUT DOWN ON THE poor-quality meats and Flintstone-size portions, meat can play a valuable role in a healthy diet. This is especially true when it comes from pasture-raised animals on sustainable farms. Meat is a great source of protein, iron, zinc, and B vitamins. But you negate those benefits if you eat only conventionally raised meat, or go nuts on enormous quantities like I did. That's the fast track to increased risk for type 2 diabetes and heart disease. I still have a weakness for slow-cooked pork, meatballs, and piles of prosciutto, but now meat is a complement, not the dominating element, in most of my meals. Besides paying attention to quantity, the keys to getting useful nutrients and vitamins and less of the artery-clogging, inflammation-inducing crap are to choose lean cuts more often and to source wisely.

Overall, meat from pasture-raised animals is leaner than that from grain-fed animals on factory farms, so the better quality the meat, the more likely it is to be better *for* you. Leaner beef options include flank steak, hanger steak, top sirloin, and top round. When shopping for pork or lamb, try tenderloin, loin chops, and leg. This may surprise you about poultry—white meat is only a smidge leaner than dark. It's certainly not enough to ban chicken thighs from your plate. There's no denying that fatty meat is freakin' tasty, but you'll find that less fat doesn't have to mean less taste. You just have to approach lean meats differently. Forget the thick steak, the 2-inch-tall burger patty, the whole roasted prime rib that's all interior meat and little sear. The trick to maximizing the flavor of lean meats is in surface area, not thickness.

My favorite way to cook a piece of meat is to develop an incredibly flavorful caramelized crust by searing it with a little salt and olive oil in a hot pan. When you increase the surface area of meat that touches the pan, you get even more caramelizing, which equals more flavor. The key is to slice or pound the meat thin, increasing the ratio of exterior meat to interior meat—this approach is useful with many cuts of meat, but it's especially suited to leaner cuts, like those in the Rosemary-Lemon Minute Steak (page 225) and the Flavor-Pounded Chicken (page 213), where you can't rely on high fat content for flavor. Yet even without a lot of fat on the meat, cooking with this method results in some tasty pan drippings. That meaty nectar gives you an opportunity to make a light, rich pan sauce to drizzle over whatever you're making. And yet *another* bonus is that slicing or pounding meat thin makes it cook faster. Good news all around.

Using this approach, I'll show you a crazy-simple, versatile technique for cooking boneless, skinless chicken breasts. Most chefs don't bother with these; the consensus is they're for people who don't mind chewing on a thick, dry cotton ball. I'm not afraid to admit I like chicken breasts, and it's because of the flavor pounding technique. If you're bored out of your skull with dry, tasteless bird, Flavor-Pounded Chicken is a revelation. The breasts are juicy, packed with bright flavor, and take about 4 minutes to cook—a dinner savior on a busy weeknight.

And one critical step that applies to every recipe here, whether it's red meat, pork, or poultry, lean or fat: Allow the meat to come to room temperature before cooking it. This promotes even and efficient cooking. Just set it on the counter, cover it, and let it sit for 20 to 30 minutes.

CHICKEN BROTH MAKES 2½ QUARTS

Homemade chicken broth is one hell of a powerful elixir. It drastically improves the flavor and nutrition of anything you use it in. It takes several hours to cook, but it's mostly hands off and requires little more than combining cold water, chicken bones/meat, and aromatic vegetables to produce a huge batch of fresh, nutrient-dense chicken broth. If you're used to store-bought broth, you'll be surprised at the enormous difference in flavor. Packaged broths, even the wholesome-sounding organic, free-range stuff, literally pale in comparison to homemade. They're thin and dull where this broth is rich and full-bodied (not to mention more affordable).

This broth forms the foundation for nearly every soup I make. It lasts about 1 week in the refrigerator and up to a couple of months in the freezer. ■

For an easy way to develop more flavor in any grain dish, use chicken broth instead of water as the grain's cooking liquid.

Freeze some of the broth in an ice cube tray and pop a few cubes into a hot pan for sautéing with vegetables.

4 pounds chicken bones (any combination of backs, necks, and feet)

2 pounds chicken wings

2 small onions, peeled and quartered

4 small carrots, cut into 1-inch pieces

4 celery stalks, cut into 1-inch pieces

½ bunch flat-leaf parsley

1 (12-ounce) can whole tomatoes, drained

1 teaspoon black peppercorns

2 bay leaves

1 In a deep 8-quart pot, combine the bones and wings. Run cold water over the chicken parts to thoroughly rinse them, using your hands to give it some dishwashing action. Drain the water and lightly pack the chicken in the pot. Cover the chicken by 4 inches with cold water and bring it to a boil over medium-high heat, 45 minutes to 1 hour.

2 As soon as the liquid boils, reduce the heat to medium and move the pot so the burner is not centered, but off to one side. (This encourages the broth to circulate over and around the meat.) Simmer, occasionally using a ladle to skim and discard any fat and foamy impurities that settle on the surface, until the broth looks clear, about 1 hour.

3 When the broth looks clear, add the onions, carrots, celery, parsley, tomatoes, peppercorns, and bay leaves and simmer for another 2 hours. Use a spider skimmer to remove and discard any large pieces of meat. Put a fine-mesh strainer over another large pot and pour the broth through it; discard the solids left in the strainer. Let the broth cool before storing.

WHY YOU SHOULDN'T PASS ON GRASS

A Comparison of Factory-Farm and Pasture-Raised Meats

I'm a firm believer in the old saying "You are what you eat." If you eat animals, you have to take this one step further. You are not only what *you* eat, you are what that cow in your cheeseburger ate, or what the chicken in your box of fried wings feasted on for lunch last week. There is a vast difference between the nutritional value of pasture-raised, humanely raised meat and the type you're most likely eating—factory-farm meat from sickly animals that ate cheap corn and grain products and were pumped with hormones and antibiotics. That's why it's incredibly important to get the highest quality meat your wallet allows. Much of what's available at American supermarkets is meat from industrial-scale factory farms that treat animals as products rather than living things. Profit is their bottom line, and little thought is given to the actual care of the animal or the environment. The bigger their profits, the more our meat supply is compromised.

Feedlot cattle and chickens are fed a diet of mostly cheap, pesticide-laced corn and other grains—they fatten up fast, similar to people shoveling down high-carb foods. In addition, cattle are often given hormones to further promote unnaturally quick growth. But the issue with cattle is that their stomachs are designed to digest grasses, not grains. This practice wreaks havoc on cows' health, so they have to be injected with antibiotics regularly. To make matters worse, these cattle, pigs, and chickens spend most of their stressful lives standing in piles of feces while packed together tighter than a subway car during morning rush hour. The variety of environmental, economic, and moral problems ensuing from this backward process is mind-boggling.

Now consider what it's like for pasture-raised animals. They roam freely while grazing on a natural diet of grass and hay. They're never given growth hormones and rarely given antibiotics. These animals are raised much closer to the way nature intended, so they're healthier. If the meat you eat comes from these animals, you're healthier too. Pasture-raised grass-fed beef is lower in overall fat than grain-fed beef, but higher in good fats like omega-3 fatty acids and conjugated linoleic acid (CLA), which help strengthen your heart and immune system. Grain-fed beef contains more omega-6 fatty acids, the type of fat that in large quantities contributes to chronic inflammation and cancer (page 174). It's not just about fat—meat and dairy from grass-fed cows have up to four times more vitamin E (another powerful heart disease– and cancer-fighter), and more vitamin A, thiamin, riboflavin, calcium, and magnesium. On the flavor front, your taste buds are primed for well-marbled corn-fed meat that explodes with fat and sweetness. But grass-fed beef is every bit as flavorful—it's more savory, earthier, just plain "beefier." I love it, and the quick technique used in the Rosemary-Lemon Minute Steak (page 225) is my favorite way to bring out its flavor.

You're far better off with pasture-fed chicken too. With more omega-3s and vitamin E, and less overall saturated fat, it is heads and shoulders above the quality of meat from grain-fed chickens in filthy feedlots. Just look at the difference between pastured chickens' bright yellow egg yolks and the murky, pale feedlot chicken yolks. Pasture-raised chickens also have more flavor than their factory-raised counterparts because they were able to munch away on a range of different natural foods, rather than synthetic food.

Unfortunately, it's not easy to know what you're getting at the grocery store. The labels on meat packaging are notoriously baffling, and some of them are just smoke-and-mirrors marketing terms rather than official certifications. Here are a number of clarifications on what these different terms mean, so you know how to shop smart for meat that not only tastes good, but is infinitely better for you:

With beef, know that even if it's USDA-Certified Organic, it's not necessarily grass-fed. Certified Organic beef means the beef comes from cattle that haven't been shot up with antibiotics or hormones and have been fed certified organic food. But that cow could have been raised on corn and other grains, which means it still has an unhealthy fat balance of more omega-6s than omega-3s. Even if cattle are fed organic grains, their meat is not as nutritious as grass-fed.

Ideally, you can purchase red meat (beef, sheep, and lamb) that's certified grass-fed by the American Grassfed Association. Your neighborhood supermarket may not carry it, so a good place to start is your local farmers' market. Ask these vendors questions. Do you raise your livestock? Is your meat hormone-and antibiotic-free? What do you feed your animals? Even if it isn't certified 100% grass-fed, meat from a trusted local farmer feeding their

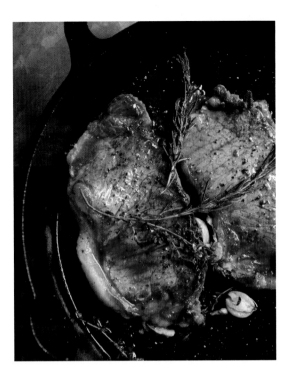

livestock grass and hay is a good choice. You can also try retail stores along the lines of Whole Foods. When buying poultry, birds labeled as USDA-Certified Organic and pastured or pasture-raised are the best option. These are easier to find in supermarkets these days. Great online resources like EatWild.org, AmericanGrass-Fed.org, and LocalHarvest.org have directories of pasture-based farms in your area. Some of them will ship the meat straight to your door.

For many people, the downside of buying pastured meat is its high price tag. It can be shocking, if you're used to buying standard-issue, grain-fed meat. My family goes the "pay more and eat less" route suggested by Michael Pollan. The price may sting, but I know I'm paying the true cost of what it takes to raise and feed animals in a healthy, ethical, environmentally sound way.

DECODING MEAT LABELING TERMS

(an asterisk indicates that this label comes from the USDA [U.S. Department of Agriculture])

*No Antibiotics Added/*Raised Without Antibiotics/Antibiotic-Free: Meat and poultry products can be labeled "no antibiotics added," "raised without antibiotics," and "no antibiotics" if the producer documents that the animals were raised without antibiotics, and that the meat is not from a sick animal treated with antibiotics. Note: The label "antibiotic-free" isn't USDA-approved, and is not allowed on meat labels.

*Cage-Free: On an egg carton, this means that the laying hens were not raised in cages, but it doesn't always mean the hens have access to the outdoors, nor does it tell you what the hens are fed. On a package of chicken, this term is meaningless—poultry raised for their meat are rarely caged.

Certified humane: The Humane Farm Animal Care, a nonprofit organization, regulates this label, and certifies that the farm animals were treated humanely—not raised in cages or crates, injected with growth hormones, or unnecessarily administered antibiotics.

*Free Range: This label on a package of chicken tells you the birds have been allowed access to the outdoors. It is not the same as pastured, because there's no requirement for the amount of time the chicken is outside, nor the quality or size of the outdoor space.

*Grass-Fed: The gold standard for this certification is from the American Grassfed Association, which says "100% grass-fed" on meat and dairy products from animals raised solely on natural grasses and hay, not grains. The USDA grass-fed label is not as comprehensive—there is a loophole allowing animals to spend part of their lives in confined pens.

Halal: Meat with the halal label is acceptable according to Islamic law, and guarantees that the animal was fed a natural diet and slaughtered in a specific way. But it does not have standards for antibiotic usage or the environment the animal is raised in.

*No Hormones Administered/Hormone-Free: This is for beef and dairy products, and can be used only if producers document that the cattle were raised without hormones. It doesn't specify if the animal received antibiotics.

Kosher: Kosher certified meat and dairy is acceptable according to Jewish dietary laws. To be kosher, the meat has to come from an animal slaughtered according to specific standards, but does not address the use of growth hormones or antibiotics.

*Natural: This term only clarifies that no artificial colors, flavors, or preservatives were added to the meat during processing.

Naturally raised: This standard clarifies "livestock used for the production of meat and meat products have been raised entirely without growth promotants, antibiotics, and have never been fed animal by-products." So you get some assurance about how the animal was fed, but you can't tell if it was raised outdoors or crammed in cages.

*Organic/*Certified Organic: This means that animals have been raised without antibiotics and hormones and that, if they were fed grains, those grains are organic. Certified organic meat must also come from animals that have at least some access to pasture. All food labeled as organic is verified by an independent organization.

Pasture-Raised/Pastured: This label implies that cattle had year-round access to a pasture. "Pasture-raised" and "100% grass-fed" are the only labels meant to give you the assurance that the animals were not fed grains, which is why many people consider these even better than "organic." However, pasture-raised is not a regulated term, so producers can use it however they like.

BONE BROTHS

I like using chicken wings in addition to chicken bones because that bit of meat boosts the flavor of the broth, and chicken wings are inexpensive and typically easier to find than chicken feet and necks. If you don't see packages of chicken bones in the meat section of your grocery store, ask the butcher—there's a good chance they have some in the back. If not, you can increase the chicken wings to 6 pounds (just make sure you use a larger pot). Besides their amazing flavor and incomparable usefulness in cooking, bone broths are powerful health tonics. You know chicken soup's reputation as a remedy for colds and the flu? There's science to back that up: Any broth made by boiling animal bones with a few vegetables and herbs has immense benefits. Bone broths are high in minerals like calcium, magnesium, and phosphorous, which are good for bones and teeth. The collagen in bone broths supports the development of healthy joints, ligaments and tendons, hair, and skin. Gelatin maximizes the effects of digestive juices, making it easier to digest protein, grains, and beans. And the reason it's particularly great when you're sick is that all the good stuff in bone broths is easily processed and absorbed by your body. Since broths are a concentrated source of animal bones, it's important that you use bones only from pasture-raised chicken, grass-fed beef, or wild-caught fish.

THAI CHICKEN COCONUT SOUP
SERVES 4 TO 6

This has that comforting, cure-all effect that I love in a chicken soup, and it's packed with rich flavor. You'll question its virtue because it's so creamy and satisfying—it just tastes too damn good to be healthy! But there's actually a bunch of beneficial stuff in here, including the great fat in coconut milk and the digestion-enhancing powers of galangal.

Galangal looks a lot like its cousin ginger, but it's denser and has a sharper flavor that tastes more like pepper. If you can't find it at your grocery, you can use ginger. It doesn't taste the same but works just as well with the other flavors in the soup. Either way, be sure to slice it as thin as possible. Whatever is leftover of your knob of galangal or ginger can be frozen, and you can just grate the frozen piece as needed. ■

The idea of sipping ginger ale to settle an upset stomach comes from ginger's power as a digestive aid. Both ginger and galangal are natural remedies for indigestion, heartburn, nausea, and other funky stomach issues. People with arthritis benefit from eating fresh ginger or galangal regularly because both have potent anti-inflammatory properties.

2 (12-ounce) cans unsweetened coconut milk

3 cups Chicken Broth (page 199)

1 stalk fresh lemongrass, cut into 3 pieces and smashed with the flat side of a knife

1 (1-inch) piece galangal, peeled and cut into about 20 thin slices

Grated zest of 1 lime

1 pound boneless, skinless chicken breasts, cut into 1½-inch-long strips

½ large onion, diced (about 1 cup)

1 small red bell pepper, diced (about 1 cup)

1 small fresh Thai chile, cut into about 15 thin slices

8 ounces white button mushrooms, quartered (about 2 cups)

½ cup fresh lime juice (4 to 5 limes)

3½ tablespoons fish sauce

2 tablespoons coconut palm sugar (optional)

⅓ cup packed cilantro leaves, plus more for garnish

1 In a large pot, combine the coconut milk, chicken broth, lemongrass, galangal slices, and lime zest and bring to a boil over high heat. Reduce the heat to medium-low and simmer for 15 minutes.

2 Add the chicken, onion, bell pepper, chile, mushrooms, lime juice, fish sauce, and coconut sugar (if using), and give it all a stir. Simmer for 15 minutes.

3 Stir in the cilantro, turn off the heat, and cover. Let it sit for 10 minutes, so the cilantro can steep. Scoop out and discard the lemongrass. To serve, ladle into bowls and top each with cilantro leaves.

JAPANESE CHICKEN AND RICE SOUP SERVES 4 TO 6

If I haven't harped enough on how advantageous it is to have homemade chicken broth on hand, this recipe should hit it home for you. In just 25 minutes, you're digging into a bowl of warming, deeply flavorful, umami-filled, immunity-boosting soup. Thin strips of chicken quickly poach in broth swimming with brown rice, toasted nori, shiitake mushrooms, tamari, and a bit of lemon juice. I find there's a lot of symmetry between Italian and Japanese cuisines, not only for their emphasis on seasonality and simplicity, but also for their heavy reliance on umami ingredients. Where Italian cooks use tomatoes, anchovies, Parmesan cheese, and dried porcinis, Japanese use soy sauce, tamari, miso paste, seaweed, and bonito flakes (dried, fermented fish).

Nori is dried seaweed, which you probably know best as the wrapper for sushi rolls. I love how it adds a hint of salty sea flavor to the earthiness of the mushrooms and the rich chicken broth. Look for toasted nori strips in the Asian food section of your store. I use Eden Foods Nori Krinkles. ■

7 cups Chicken Broth (page 199)

1 pound boneless, skinless chicken breasts, thinly sliced into 1-inch-long pieces

1 teaspoon finely grated fresh ginger

3½ ounces fresh shiitake mushrooms, stems discarded, caps thinly sliced (about 1½ cups)

1 cup cooked brown rice

½ cup nori crinkles (or you can slice up your own toasted nori sheets into ½-inch squares)

2 tablespoons tamari

Juice of ½ lemon

1 bunch scallions, white and pale green parts only, thinly sliced (about ½ cup)

1 In a large pot, bring the chicken broth to a boil over high heat. In a small bowl, combine the chicken and ginger and mix well.

2 When the broth reaches a boil, bring the heat down to medium. Add the ginger-marinated chicken and give it a stir. Add the shiitakes, rice, nori, tamari, and lemon juice and stir. Cover and cook for 5 minutes. Stir in the scallions. Ladle into bowls and serve.

Tamari is a staple in most Asian pantries. It looks and tastes a lot like soy sauce, since they're both made from fermented soybeans. The difference is that soy sauce is almost always made with wheat and tamari is traditionally made with little or no wheat. Tamari's rich concentration of soybeans gives it a darker color and deeper, smoother flavor than soy sauce. It's also less salty, so I prefer it to soy sauce for cooking.

MEXICAN CHICKEN SOUP SERVES 4 TO 6

This lively chicken soup relies on the essential Mexican flavors of corn, lime, cilantro, avocado, and jalapeño. The heat from the jalapeño is fairly mild, so if you like things with more assertive heat, add another jalapeño and leave in the seeds. The chicken here comes from pan-roasted, bone-in, skin-on chicken breasts; the bone and skin contribute immensely to the flavor and moistness of the chicken. Cooking meat on the bone helps even the distribution of heat and the skin protects the exterior so it doesn't dry out before the inside is cooked. You can use this simple method to roast a few pounds of bone-in, skin-on chicken breasts and keep the meat around for soups, sandwiches, and quick snacks. ■

2 pounds bone-in, skin-on chicken breasts, rinsed and patted dry

Fine sea salt and freshly ground black pepper

3 tablespoons extra virgin olive oil

1 cup chopped carrots

2 cups chopped celery

2 cups chopped onion

1 fresh jalapeño pepper, seeded and minced

2 tomatoes, halved, juiced, and roughly chopped or 1 (14.5-ounce) can whole tomatoes, drained and chopped (about 2 cups)

1 cup fresh or frozen corn kernels

7 cups Chicken Broth (page 199)

¼ cup chopped fresh cilantro

1 tablespoon fresh lime juice

2 avocados

Thinly sliced radishes, cilantro leaves, and lime wedges, for serving (optional)

1 Let the chicken come to room temperature about 20 minutes before cooking. Preheat the oven to 425°F. Generously season the chicken on both sides.

2 In an ovenproof skillet, heat 1 tablespoon of the olive oil over high heat. When the oil slides easily across the pan, add the chicken skin-side down and cook, untouched, for 1 minute. Transfer the skillet to the oven and cook until the chicken shows no sign of pink when pierced near the bone, about 30 minutes. Flip each breast and set the skillet aside until the chicken is cool enough to handle. Chop or shred the meat into bite-size pieces, discarding the skin and bones.

3 In a large pot, heat the remaining 2 tablespoons olive oil over high heat. When the oil is hot, add the carrots, celery, onions, and jalapeño. Stir and cook for 1 minute. Reduce the heat to medium, cover, and cook for 10 minutes, stirring occasionally. Add the tomatoes, corn, and a few pinches of salt. Cover and cook, stirring occasionally, until the tomatoes start to soften, about 5 minutes. Add the broth and bring it to a boil over high heat, then reduce the heat and simmer for 15 minutes. Add the chicken, cilantro, and lime juice and simmer for 5 minutes.

4 To serve, scoop one-quarter of an avocado into each bowl and chop it up into a few chunks. Ladle the soup over it and add any of the toppings you like.

NEW YORK CITY JEWISH-STYLE CHICKEN SOUP SERVES 4 TO 6

Classic Jewish chicken soup is a glorious thing. For me, it's up there with ribollita (my favorite Tuscan soup, page 119) as one of the best ways to fully appreciate the simplicity and beauty of broth-based soup. My version takes cues from the many bowls I dug into over the years at the original 2nd Ave Deli, one of New York City's most famous Jewish delis. I roast bone-in, skin-on chicken breasts and add the meat to a golden pool of chicken broth, along with dill and chunks of carrots, celery, and onion. After consulting my Hebrew helper, an expert on the matter, I also worked in the Jewish "golden coins." Traditionally, these are dollops of chicken fat that rise to the top of the soup and don't get skimmed off. My nod to the fatty goodness of the golden coins is to top each serving with generous dots of extra virgin olive oil. ∎

2 pounds bone-in, skin-on chicken breasts, rinsed and patted dry

Fine sea salt and freshly ground black pepper

3 tablespoons extra virgin olive oil, plus more for garnish

2 large carrots, halved lengthwise and cut crosswise into ¼-inch-thick slices (about 2 cups)

4 celery stalks, chopped (about 1½ cups)

1 large onion, cut into large dice (about 2 cups)

7 cups Chicken Broth (page 199)

2 tablespoons chopped fresh dill

1 Let the chicken come to room temperature about 20 minutes before cooking. Preheat the oven to 425°F. Generously season the chicken on both sides with salt and pepper.

2 In a large ovenproof skillet, heat 1 tablespoon of the olive oil over high heat. When the oil slides easily across the pan, add the chicken skin-side down and cook, untouched, for 1 minute. Transfer the skillet to the oven and cook until the chicken shows no sign of pink when pierced near the bone, about 30 minutes. Flip each breast and set the skillet aside until the chicken is cool enough to handle. Chop or shred the meat into bite-size pieces (these can go back into the skillet), discarding the skin and bones.

3 In a large pot, heat the remaining 2 tablespoons olive oil over high heat. When the oil shimmers, add the carrots, celery, onion, and a pinch of salt and cook for 1 minute. Reduce the heat to medium, cover, and cook for 15 minutes, stirring occasionally. Pour in the chicken broth and bring to a boil. Reduce the heat and simmer until the vegetables are tender about 15 minutes. Add the chicken (including the juices it released in the skillet) and dill and simmer for 5 minutes more. Add salt to taste.

4 To serve, ladle into bowls and dot the top of each serving with a couple of ½-teaspoon "golden coins" of olive oil.

FLAVOR-POUNDED CHICKEN SERVES 4

For years I had zero respect for boneless, skinless chicken breasts and questioned why anyone bothered with a food so bland and oppressively dry that eating it feels like chewing on a towel. But as I set off on the path to eat better, I couldn't help but come face-to-face with boneless, skinless chicken breasts. They're lean, full of protein, versatile, and, as it turns out, capable of carrying a ton of flavor and juiciness if you cook them right. To do this, I butterfly the breast and pound the meat thin, so it cooks evenly and quickly without drying out. This also increases the surface area of meat touching the pan, leading to that deeply flavorful crust I want. Then I make a mixture of Tuscan flavors—olive oil, chopped sage and rosemary, lemon, and garlic—and literally pound it directly into both sides of the breast. After just 90 seconds in a hot pan, the payoff is an insanely tender, delicious chicken breast that has all the succulence of dark meat. Another perk to this method is that the size of the thinned-out meat tricks you into thinking you're getting a lot more than just one breast. (When your plate looks full, you tend to believe you're eating more and feel full as a result.)

The best results come from smaller chicken breasts—they're easier to pound out to a uniform thickness. You can easily prepare the breasts ahead of time—after step 2, just cover the chicken in plastic wrap and refrigerate, and they'll keep for up to 2 days. You can also cook more than one at a time, but be sure you don't overcrowd the pan, or you'll have a hard time developing a caramelized crust. ■

4 (6- to 8-ounce) boneless, skinless chicken breasts

12 large fresh sage leaves, roughly chopped

Leaves from 2 sprigs of fresh rosemary, roughly chopped

Grated zest of 2 small lemons

2 small garlic cloves, roughly chopped

1 tablespoon fine sea salt

Freshly ground black pepper

8 teaspoons extra virgin olive oil, plus 4 tablespoons for cooking

4 lemon wedges

1 Starting at the thicker side, make a lengthwise cut into the top two-thirds of a chicken breast, stopping before cutting all the way through. Fold it open like a book. (The chicken breast should still be in one piece.) Put the breast between two pieces of plastic wrap and pound it out on both sides with the flat side of a meat tenderizer, working from the inside out, until it's spread to double its original size and about ¼ inch thick. Repeat with the remaining breasts.

2 Pile the sage, rosemary, lemon zest, and garlic on a cutting board and chop together until blended. In a bowl, combine the herb mixture, salt, a few grinds of black pepper, and 8 teaspoons of the olive oil. Divide half of the herb paste evenly across one side of the 4 chicken breasts and rub it in. Cover with plastic wrap again and lightly pound in the seasoning with the toothy side of the meat tenderizer. Flip the breasts, rub the remaining herb paste into the other side of the chicken breasts. Cover with plastic wrap and lightly pound in the seasoning.

RECIPE CONTINUES

Butterfly the breast, making a lengthwise cut into the top two-thirds.

Cover the meat with plastic wrap and pound on both sides with the flat side of a meat tenderizer.

Unwrap and add the seasoning, then rewrap and pound with the toothy side of the meat tenderizer.

3 In a large skillet heat 1 tablespoon of the olive oil over high heat. Wait 2 minutes, or until it's smoking hot, add 1 chicken breast, put a weight on it (a teakettle or heavy pan) and cook for 45 seconds. Flip, add the weight, and cook for another 45 seconds. Transfer to a plate, and let it rest for 3 minutes. Meanwhile, repeat with the remaining chicken breasts. Squeeze a wedge of lemon over each flavor-pounded chicken just before serving.

Variations

While Tuscan flavors are my natural inclination, I often make one of the Flavor-Pounded Chicken variations below. Except for the couple instances that I've noted, steps 1 and 3 are the same for all. Once you get an understanding of the process, I encourage you to follow your own preferences and start pounding whatever flavor you like into the chicken.

INDIAN

2 teaspoons ground cumin

2 teaspoons turmeric

2 teaspoons onion powder

2 teaspoons ground coriander

1 tablespoon fine sea salt

Freshly ground black pepper

2 teaspoons extra virgin olive oil

For step 2: In a bowl, combine the cumin, turmeric, onion powder, coriander, salt, several grinds of pepper, and the olive oil. Season and pound as described in the main recipe.

MAPLE SPICE

2 teaspoons ground cinnamon

2 teaspoons freshly grated nutmeg

2 teaspoons ground ginger

1 tablespoon fine sea salt

Freshly ground black pepper

4 teaspoons maple syrup

For step 2: In a bowl, combine the cinnamon, nutmeg, ginger, salt, and several grinds of pepper. Divide half the spice mixture evenly across one side of the 4 chicken breasts and drizzle ½ teaspoon maple syrup over each. Rub in the seasoning and maple syrup. Cover with plastic wrap and lightly pound in the seasoning with the toothy side of the meat tenderizer. Flip and rub the rest of the spice mixture into the other side of the chicken breasts. Drizzle another ½ teaspoon maple syrup over each breast. Cover with plastic wrap and lightly pound in the seasoning.

ITALIAN-AMERICAN

2 teaspoons garlic powder

2 teaspoons dried oregano

1 tablespoon fine sea salt

4 teaspoons grated Parmigiano-Reggiano cheese

Freshly ground black pepper

4 teaspoons extra virgin olive oil

2 teaspoons tomato paste

Indian

Italian-American

Japanese

For step 2: In a bowl, combine the garlic powder, oregano, salt, Parmesan, several grinds of pepper, and the olive oil. Divide half the oregano mixture evenly across one side of the 4 chicken breasts and add ¼ teaspoon tomato paste to each breast. Rub in the seasoning and tomato paste. Cover with plastic wrap and lightly pound in the seasoning with the toothy side of the meat tenderizer. Flip and divide the rest of the oregano mixture evenly across the other side of the chicken breasts. Add another ¼ teaspoon of tomato paste to each breast and rub it in. Cover with plastic wrap before lightly pounding again.

THAI
Grated zest of 4 limes

2 teaspoons grated fresh ginger

4 teaspoons chopped fresh cilantro

1 teaspoon ground cardamom

1 tablespoon fine sea salt

2 teaspoons fish sauce

2 teaspoons tamarind paste (optional)

4 tablespoons virgin coconut oil

4 lime wedges

For step 2: In a bowl, combine the lime zest, ginger, cilantro, cardamom, salt, fish sauce, and tamarind paste (if using). Divide half the mixture evenly across one side of the 4 chicken breasts and rub it in. Cover with plastic wrap and lightly pound in the seasoning with the toothy side of the meat tenderizer. Flip and rub the rest of the mixture into the other side of the chicken breasts. Cover with plastic wrap and lightly pound in the seasoning.

For step 3: Substitute coconut oil for olive oil and squeeze a wedge of lime over each flavor-pounded chicken just before serving.

JAPANESE
Grated zest of 2 lemons

2 teaspoons grated fresh ginger

2 teaspoons dried seaweed granules (dulse, kelp, nori, any kind works)

4 teaspoons soy sauce or tamari

4 teaspoons toasted sesame oil

1 tablespoon fine sea salt

For step 2: In a bowl, combine the lemon zest, ginger, seaweed granules, soy sauce, sesame oil, and salt. Season and pound as described in the main recipe.

Flavor-Pounded Chicken is excellent over greens. Toss arugula and sliced red onions with balsamic vinegar and extra virgin olive oil. Make a bed of salad on a plate and top it with an FPC. The residual heat from the chicken works its way into the greens and does something magical.

HERB-ROASTED SPATCHCOCK CHICKEN SERVES 4

I'm all about spatchcocking— it is hands down my favorite technique for roasting a chicken. In a lot less time than it takes to cook a whole bird, you get evenly cooked, ridiculously tender, moist chicken with all-over browned, crispy skin. By removing the backbone and the breastbone (called the keel bone), the bird lies flat, more skin is exposed to the heat, and it's easier to cut into pieces than a whole, intact bird. A quick pan-sear before roasting gives the skin a deep brown color, and a simple lemon and garlic pan sauce is a nice finishing touch. I like cast iron for this because it holds heat well and evenly, but you can use a regular 12-inch pan if that's what you have. ∎

CHICKEN

1 (3½- to 4-pound) whole chicken

1½ tablespoons chopped fresh rosemary

Grated zest of 2 lemons

1 garlic clove, finely grated

3 tablespoons extra virgin olive oil

Fine sea salt and freshly ground black pepper

PAN SAUCE

3 garlic cloves, peeled and cracked

1 sprig of fresh rosemary

Juice of 1 lemon

Red pepper flakes (optional)

1 Let the chicken come to room temperature 30 minutes before you're ready to cook. Put a 12-inch cast iron skillet in the oven and heat it to 425°F.

2 Combine the rosemary, lemon zest, and garlic on a cutting board and finely chop together. In a small bowl, combine the herb mixture, 1 tablespoon olive oil, ½ teaspoon salt, and about 10 grinds of pepper into a paste.

3 Rinse and pat dry with paper towels. Put the chicken breast-side down on a cutting board with the neck end closest to

you. Trim any excess skin and fat from the opening of the neck cavity. Remove the backbone by cutting along each side of it from the neck to the tail.

4 To remove the keel bone (the breastbone), press the chicken open wider to expose the cavity. At the neck end, use the heel of a sharp knife to make a 1-inch cut on both sides of the keel bone. Bend the bird back, splaying it open like a book. Cut the membrane along the center of the chicken to expose the keel bone and cartilage. Run your thumbs up and under both sides of the cartilage until it separates from the breast. Gradually pull out the cartilage and keel bone.

5 Flip the chicken over breast-side up and use your index finger to loosen the skin of the drumsticks, thighs, and breasts. Tuck the herb paste under the skin, spreading it into an even layer by pressing and pushing it around from the top of the skin.

6 Take the hot skillet out of the oven and continue to heat it on the stovetop over high heat. Generously season both sides of the chicken with salt and pepper. Add the remaining 2 tablespoons olive oil to the pan and swirl it

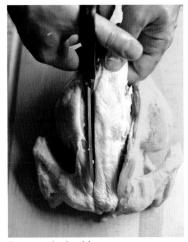

Remove the backbone.

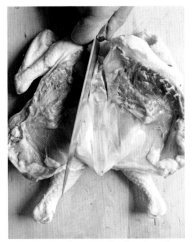

Make a 1-inch cut on both sides of the keel bone.

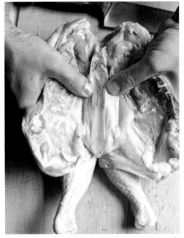

Run your thumbs under both sides of the cartilage.

around to coat. Put the chicken in skin-side down, cook for 3 minutes, then transfer it to the oven. Roast for 30 minutes. To check for doneness, poke the thickest part of the thigh with a fork. If the juices run clear, it's done. If they're pink, roast for 5 more minutes. If the skin hasn't crisped up, cook it on the stove over high heat for 2 minutes. Transfer the chicken to a large plate to rest for 10 minutes.

7 For the pan sauce: Add the garlic, rosemary, and lemon juice to the pan and put it over high heat (throw in red pepper flakes for a little spice). Scrape the bottom to loosen the caramelized bits of chicken. Spoon any chicken juices that have released on the plate into the pan. Cook for 3 minutes. Pour the sauce over the chicken and serve.

BRAISED CHICKEN THIGHS WITH GARLIC, LEMON, AND GREEK OLIVES SERVES 4

This easy one-pot dinner is all about chicken thighs, the underdog of the poultry world. The thighs' dark, nutrient-dense meat is undeniably richer, juicier, and more tender than white meat. Also, high demand for boneless, skinless chicken breasts means the deep flavor and juicy potential of the chicken thighs comes at an unbelievable value. Thighs on the bone are a forgiving cut that can take the heat without drying out, so the meat turns out meltingly soft and juicy. The lemon slices cook down in the liquid gold of the chicken fat and juice, infusing the whole dish with bright flavor that balances the richness of the meat. This comes together in about an hour and is simple enough for a weeknight dinner, and fancy enough to serve to guests. ∎

Yes, dark meat has more fat than white meat, but the difference is minimal—about 1 gram per ounce. Dark meat also delivers considerably more iron and B vitamins and twice the amount of zinc as white meat.

The olives provide saltiness here, so go easy on the salt in steps 1 and 3.

8 bone-in, skin-on chicken thighs

Fine sea salt and freshly ground black pepper

3 tablespoons extra virgin olive oil

12 garlic cloves, peeled

2 large yellow onions, thinly sliced (about 4 cups)

1 lemon, thinly sliced and seeds discarded

2 tablespoons fresh oregano leaves, plus more for garnish

1 cup mixed Greek olives

Juice of 1 lemon

1 Let the chicken come to room temperature about 20 minutes before cooking. Preheat the oven to 350°F. Season the chicken on both sides with salt and pepper.

2 In an ovenproof pan (a 3.5-quart braiser or Dutch oven) large enough to hold all the thighs in a single layer, heat the olive oil over high heat. When the pan is hot and the oil slides easily across the pan, add the thighs skin-side down. Resist the urge to move them around, allowing them to cook untouched until you get a nice, golden brown sear on the skin, 5 to 6 minutes. Add the garlic cloves to the pan and flip each thigh over. Cook until the garlic has taken on some browning, about 3 minutes. Remove the chicken and garlic from the pan and set on a plate.

3 With the pan still over high heat, add the onions, lemon slices, oregano, and salt and pepper to taste. Stir to coat everything in the oil and loosen up the browned bits on the bottom of the pan. Cook for 5 minutes. Nestle the thighs skin-side up in the onion mixture and add the cooked garlic cloves and the olives. Squeeze the lemon juice over the chicken and transfer the pan to the oven to bake for 40 minutes. Scatter fresh oregano leaves over the top and serve.

GRASS-FED BEEF MEATLOAF WITH ROASTED BROCCOLI, CARROT, AND ONION SERVES 6

I love meatballs, so it's pretty obvious I love meatloaf too. It's so hit or miss, though—when it's good, meatloaf is moist, light, well seasoned, and made with high-quality beef. When it's not (and it's usually not), it's a heavy, breadcrumb-loaded, flavorless lump of feedlot beef blanketed in sugary ketchup. On my elusive quest for meatloaf that delivers on flavor and texture without relying on carbs or high-fructose condiments, I've come up with a few tricks. First, I use a mixture of ground flaxseed and milk to bind everything together in the meatloaf. It acts just like breadcrumbs, without the white flour or gluten. I also add a mixture of sautéed minced vegetables to give moisture to the meat as it cooks, which prevents it from entering dense, dry territory. To lighten up the earthy beef flavor, I work in bright flavor from herbs and lemon zest. And finally, rather than cook it in a loaf pan, I shape the loaf freeform on a baking sheet to encourage a nice brown crust on all sides. If there are leftovers, I highly recommend cold meatloaf sandwiches for lunch. ■

MEATLOAF

2 pounds 100% grass-fed ground beef

⅓ cup ground flaxseeds

½ cup whole milk

1 medium red onion, roughly chopped (about 1 cup)

1 large carrot, roughly chopped (about ½ cup)

1 celery stalk, roughly chopped (about ½ cup)

4 garlic cloves, roughly chopped (about 2 tablespoons)

1 tablespoon roughly chopped fresh rosemary

1 tablespoon roughly chopped fresh sage

2 tablespoons roughly chopped fresh flat-leaf parsley

Peel of 1 lemon

2 tablespoons extra virgin olive oil

¼ cup freshly grated Parmigiano-Reggiano cheese

1½ tablespoons fine sea salt

Freshly ground black pepper

2 extra-large eggs

VEGETABLES

1 head broccoli

1 small yellow onion

4 small carrots, peeled (if bigger than ½ inch in diameter, halve them lengthwise)

2 tablespoons extra virgin olive oil

Leaves from 1 sprig of fresh sage, roughly torn

Leaves from 1 sprig of fresh rosemary

Fine sea salt and freshly ground black pepper

1 For the meatloaf: Let the meat come to room temperature about 20 minutes before cooking. Preheat the oven to 350°F. Line a 12 × 18-inch baking sheet with foil. In a bowl, combine the ground flaxseeds and milk and set aside.

2 In a food processor, combine the red onion, carrot, celery, garlic, herbs, and lemon peel and pulse just until everything is minced (not too long or you'll get a pureed, watery mixture).

3 In a 10-inch skillet, heat the olive oil over high heat. When you see wisps of smoke coming off the pan, add the minced vegetable mixture and cook for 3 minutes to soften them and bring out more flavor. Set the skillet aside to let the mixture cool.

4 In a large bowl, combine the beef, Parmesan, flaxseed-milk mixture, salt, a good dose of pepper (about 25 grinds), and the eggs. Add the cooled vegetable mixture. Using your hands, mix just long enough to incorporate everything together (do not overwork the meat).

5 Moisten your hands a little so the meat won't stick to them. On a 12 × 18-inch baking sheet, form the meat into a loaf shape about 12 inches long × 5 inches wide × 2 inches tall.

6 For the vegetables: Trim the broccoli and cut it lengthwise into spears so the stalk and florets stay intact as little trees. Halve the yellow onion from root to tip, then cut each half lengthwise into 5 wedges. In a large bowl, combine the broccoli, onion, carrots, olive oil, and herbs. Add salt and pepper to taste, then toss to combine. Scatter the vegetables in a single layer around the meatloaf (it's okay if they're crowded).

7 Bake the meatloaf for 45 minutes. Flip the vegetables and bake until the meatloaf is browned and an instant-read thermometer inserted in the center reads 150°F, about another 30 minutes. Remove from the oven and let the meatloaf rest for 15 minutes before slicing.

MIXED VEGETABLES AND HERBS
FOR MEATLOAF (PAGE 220)

GINGER-SCALLION TURKEY BURGERS MAKES 6 PATTIES

Despite their fast-food association, there's nothing inherently "bad" about burgers. It's the lackluster quality of meat, processed white flour buns, and mountains of cheese and sugary ketchup that muck things up. I've always been a beef hamburger kind of guy, but I've recently come to appreciate turkey burgers in their own right. Despite those crumbly, dried-out hockey-puck versions you may have tried, turkey burgers CAN be juicy! The key to maximum juiciness is to use ground turkey thigh meat, not just white meat. The thigh's dark meat and higher fat content give it a richer flavor. Not only is turkey leaner than beef, its milder flavor is an advantage because any fresh herbs and spices you add to it will really come through in the finished burger. So while I may be a purist with beef burgers, I like my turkey burgers to be decked out with a few flavorful mix-ins. My favorites among them are the bold Asian flavors of ginger, scallions, garlic, and soy sauce. ∎

Form your patties no thicker than ½ inch, so you have more surface area to sear and caramelize. Wet your hands with a little water before forming patties, so the meat doesn't stick.

1 pound ground turkey, preferably thigh meat

3 tablespoons minced scallions, white and pale green parts only

1 teaspoon grated fresh ginger

½ teaspoon grated garlic (about 1 medium clove)

2 teaspoons soy sauce or tamari

Fine sea salt

Extra virgin olive oil

1 In a large bowl, combine the turkey, scallions, ginger, garlic, and soy sauce. Using a rubber spatula or your hands, combine all the ingredients.

2 Form the mixture into 6 (½-inch-thick) patties, about ⅓ cup of mixture per patty. Season each patty with salt on both sides.

3 In a large skillet, heat just enough olive oil to cover the bottom over high heat. When the oil slides easily across the pan, put the patties in. Avoid overcrowding by cooking in batches, if needed. Cook for 2½ minutes without pressing on or moving the patties. Then flip the patties over and cook for another 2½ minutes on the other side.

Variations

Here are three more flavor combinations to take for a spin in your turkey burgers. The ingredients are for step 1, and steps 2 and 3 are the same as the main recipe. Combine all ingredients with the turkey and pick up the recipe above at step 2.

TUSCAN
Grated zest of 1 lemon

1 teaspoon finely chopped fresh rosemary

1 teaspoon finely chopped fresh sage

1 teaspoon grated garlic

1 teaspoon fine sea salt

Freshly ground black pepper, to taste

2 tablespoons freshly grated Parmigiano-Reggiano cheese (optional)

INDIAN
1 tablespoon finely chopped fresh mint

2 teaspoons finely chopped fresh cilantro

1½ teaspoons garam masala

1 teaspoon fine sea salt

MEXICAN
Grated zest of 1 lime

1 tablespoon finely chopped fresh cilantro

1½ teaspoons chili powder

1 teaspoon fine sea salt

ROSEMARY-LEMON MINUTE STEAK SERVES 4

These juicy steaks are an outstanding way to experience the great, clean, earthy flavor of 100% grass-fed beef. Since they have less fat than conventional grain-fed beef, grass-fed steaks call for a cooking technique similar to Flavor-Pounded Chicken (page 213). For best results, give the meat a light pounding to tenderize it and create more surface area to be exposed to the pan. This allows you to cook the steaks fast in a ripping hot pan, so they stay juicy and take on more flavor through searing. Be sure to give the pan enough time to get hot before putting the steaks in—it's essential to forming a nicely caramelized crust. ■

4 (4-ounce) grass-fed sirloin steaks, about ½ inch thick

Fine sea salt and freshly ground black pepper

3 tablespoons extra virgin olive oil

4 garlic cloves, peeled and cracked

2 sprigs of fresh rosemary

Juice of 2 small lemons

1 Pound each steak lightly with the heel of your hand to thin them out. Season the steaks with salt and pepper on both sides.

2 In a 10-inch skillet, combine 2 tablespoons of the olive oil and 2 of the garlic cloves, and turn the heat to high. When the oil slides easily across the pan, add 2 of the steaks and cook for 1 minute. Flip them over, add 1 sprig of rosemary to the pan and cook for 1 minute more. Transfer the steaks, rosemary, and garlic to a serving platter to rest. Add the remaining 1 tablespoon olive oil to the pan along with the remaining 2 garlic cloves. Cook the last 2 steaks the same way, adding the remaining sprig of rosemary after they're flipped. Turn off the heat and transfer the steaks to the serving platter to rest, leaving the garlic cloves and rosemary in the pan.

3 While the steaks rest, add the lemon juice and ¼ cup water to the pan with the cooked garlic and rosemary. Scrape the bottom with a spatula to loosen up any browned bits, and add in any juice the steaks have released onto the plate while resting. Pour the pan sauce over the steaks and serve immediately.

LIVER AND ONIONS SERVES 4

Sweet and rich, a tender piece of calf's liver can be an incomparably delicious comfort food, especially when served with a tangle of caramelized onions. That's exactly what you get with this dish, and it all happens in one pan in less than 30 minutes. There's no denying that liver has a seriously strong, distinctive flavor, but by complementing it with sweet, slow-cooked onions, aromatic herbs like rosemary and sage, and a splash of balsamic vinegar, liver becomes a thing of pleasure. I like slicing the onions into rings for this—it calls for peeling the onion without cutting it in half, but it's totally worth it for upping the visual appeal of the dish (liver needs all the help it can get). Creamy Amaranth "Polenta" with Tuscan Kale (page 162) is the perfect sidekick for this. ■

If you want to add the healthiest meats to your diet, it pays to be adventurous. Like other organ meats, liver is up there with vegetables and fruit as a treasure trove of essential vitamins and minerals. It's a potent source of iron, which helps boost your energy levels, and it's high in folate—a B vitamin that's key for cell growth.

2 tablespoons extra virgin olive oil

1 pound grass-fed calf's liver, rinsed, patted dry, and sliced into 6 pieces

Fine sea salt and freshly ground black pepper

3 onions, peeled and sliced into ¼-inch rings (leave the root end intact, so it holds the onion together as you cut it into rings)

1 tablespoon fresh rosemary leaves

1 tablespoon roughly torn fresh sage leaves

2 tablespoons balsamic vinegar

1 In a large skillet, heat 1 tablespoon of the olive oil over high heat. Season the liver on both sides with salt and pepper. When the pan is smoking hot, add the liver and sear for 1 minute on each side. Leaving the pan on the burner, use tongs to transfer the liver pieces to a plate.

2 As soon as the liver comes out, add the remaining 1 tablespoon olive oil and the onions to the pan and reduce the heat to medium-high. Cook without stirring for 3 minutes. Add the rosemary, sage, and salt and pepper to taste. Continue cooking, stirring every 3 minutes, until the onions are golden brown and caramelized, about 17 minutes. If the onions start to look dry or begin turning black in places, reduce the heat.

3 As soon as the onions are caramelized, turn the heat up to high. Wait 1 minute, then add the liver pieces back to the pan along with the balsamic vinegar. Toss everything together and turn off the heat. Let the pan sit on the stove for 5 minutes so the liver continues to cook in the residual heat. To serve, top the liver slices with the onions and pan sauce.

PORK MEDALLIONS WITH FENNEL–WHITE WINE SAUCE SERVES 4

I'll admit I was a bit of a trash-talker when it came to pork tenderloin. I found it beyond boring, the boneless, skinless chicken breast of the pork world. As I started adding more lean cuts of meat to my routine, I felt compelled to come up with a way to nudge pork tenderloin into the realm of the delicious, tender, juicy meats I love. This simple recipe nailed it. I give the tenderloin a Tuscan treatment via a quick pan sauce that includes fennel and a finely chopped mixture of rosemary, sage, and garlic. To compensate for the lack of fat in tenderloin, I slice it into medallions to increase the amount of pork touching the pan (more browning = more flavor), and cook it hard and fast. The last thing you want to do is cook the tenderloin whole or in thick steaks, which have far more bland interior meat than the seared, browned, caramelized meat you want. ■

1 large garlic clove, peeled

1 tablespoon roughly chopped fresh rosemary

1 tablespoon roughly chopped fresh sage

3 tablespoons extra virgin olive oil

1 pound pork tenderloin, cut into ½-inch-thick medallions

Fine sea salt and freshly ground black pepper

½ large fennel bulb, cut into small dice

¼ cup dry white wine

¼ cup Chicken Broth (page 199)

1 Smash the garlic clove with the flat side of a knife and roughly chop it. Combine the rosemary, sage, and garlic on the cutting board and finely chop them together.

2 In a 12-inch skillet, heat 2 tablespoons of the olive oil over high heat. While the oil heats up, season both sides of the pork medallions with salt and pepper. When the oil is smoking hot, add the medallions in one layer and cook, untouched, for 1½ minutes. Flip each medallion and cook until they're nicely browned, another 1½ minutes. Transfer the pork to a plate to rest.

3 Add the remaining 1 table-spoon olive oil to the pan (still over high heat), add the fennel, and season with salt. Cook for 1 minute, using a wooden spoon or rubber spatula to scrape up the browned bits of pork on the bottom as it cooks. Add the garlic and herb mixture, toss with the fennel, and cook for 30 seconds. Pour in the white wine, chicken broth, and any juices the pork has released on the plate. Boil for 1½ minutes, until there's only about 2 tablespoons of liquid left. Spoon the pan sauce over the pork and serve.

LAMB STEW SERVES 6

Grass-fed lamb is a great alternative to beef—it's tender, just as versatile, and can be very lean when trimmed well. The smell of lamb simmering with Indian spices and hearty, aromatic vegetables is intoxicating. The size of the vegetables for your stew is a matter of preference—big, chunky pieces or a small dice—either way works. Plain Greek yogurt is a surprise ingredient here; it adds tangy richness and thickens the broth. It seems like a minor addition, but I wouldn't make this without it. ■

Feel free to substitute veal stew meat or boneless chicken thighs here.

2 pounds grass-fed lamb stew meat, trimmed of excess fat

Fine sea salt and freshly ground black pepper

3 to 4 tablespoons extra virgin olive oil

2 small yellow onions, roughly chopped (about 1½ cups)

3 small carrots, roughly chopped (about 1 cup)

2 small Japanese or regular sweet potatoes, cut into 1-inch cubes (about 3 cups)

2 teaspoons ground coriander

1 teaspoon ground cumin

½ teaspoon turmeric

2 bay leaves

3 large garlic cloves, finely chopped

1-inch piece fresh ginger, peeled and finely chopped

1 (14.5-ounce) can diced tomatoes

¼ cup full-fat plain Greek yogurt

1 cup frozen peas

1 Let the lamb come to room temperature about 20 minutes before cooking. Season the lamb with salt and pepper.

2 Pour 3 tablespoons of the olive oil in a large saucepan or Dutch oven and turn the heat to high. When you see wisps of smoke from the pan, add half the lamb and cook without touching it for 2 minutes. Turn each piece and cook for 2 minutes more. Transfer the lamb to a bowl to rest. Repeat with the remaining lamb.

3 Add the onions, carrots, sweet potatoes, and a big pinch of salt to the same pan. (There should be a little fat still in the pan, but if it seems dry, add another tablespoon of olive oil.) Reduce the heat to medium-high and cook, stirring occasionally, until the onions are translucent and begin to take on a little browning, about 5 minutes. Add the spices, bay leaves, garlic, and ginger and cook for about 3 minutes, stirring to coat the vegetables.

4 Return the lamb to the pan along with the tomatoes and just enough water to cover the lamb and vegetables, about 2 cups. Increase the heat to high and bring to a boil. Reduce the heat to a low simmer, then cover with the lid slightly ajar, and simmer, stirring a couple of times, until the lamb is tender and the stew has thickened, about 1 hour.

5 Stir in the yogurt and peas, cover with the lid slightly ajar, and cook for 15 minutes more. Season with salt and pepper to taste.

SNACKS

SNACKS CAN BE A DOUBLE-EDGED sword. They're good for keeping energy levels up and preventing you from overeating at your next meal, but they're also notorious for wrecking an otherwise good food day. Most easy-to-reach-for snack foods are processed, junky, and full of simple carbs—the kind of food that leads you to nail a meal's worth of calories in a few minutes without realizing it.

Chips, crackers, cookies, muffins, even so-called "healthy" snacks like granola bars and organic cheese puffs, are often engineered by big food companies to be addictive. Teams of people in lab coats are creating food that piles on sugar, salt, and fat to a degree of maximum flavor they call "the bliss point." I used to get blissed out on a package of Chips Ahoy cookies on my way home from work, polishing off an entire sleeve as a "snack." Because it was full of sugar, it did nothing to stave off my hunger, so I kept on eating. Those moments are rarer now, but there are still times when I'm drawn to the salty snack aisle at the bodega across the street from Hearth. Before I know it, I purchase and tear into a bag of cheese Doritos, and once I start eating them, there's no stopping until the bag is empty. They are designed to have that exact effect: If processed foods are in the mix, snacking is almost guaranteed to get out of hand.

These days, my first line of defense against destructive snacking habits is making smart food choices for my main meals. I find that when I fill up on protein, fiber, and good fats, I don't have to rely on snacks often. I also don't raid the fridge every time I feel the slightest hunger pang. I think this contributes to a lack of consciousness about what true hunger feels like, and it kick-starts constant snacking.

My other snack strategy is preparation. On work nights, my dinner is usually early-bird style, about 5 p.m. By the time Hearth's dinner service is over six hours later, I'm starving. I don't do meals at that hour anymore, but I still need something to take the edge off my hunger before going to bed. This is when it pays to be prepared with snacks like the ones here. Being hungry without a quality snack on hand leads to crazy impulse choices like vending machine garbage, the pint of ice cream in the fridge, or the cookies and ham-

and-potato-chip sandwiches I used to fatten up on.

While things like carrot sticks and plain raw almonds are quality snacks, these don't usually cut it for me. I need something with big flavor and a combination of nutrients like healthy fats, protein, and fiber from complex carbohydrates to quiet the rumble of hunger. A small portion of last night's dinner leftovers is one of my favorite snacks—a few bites of roasted broccoli with a nugget of roast chicken or several spoonfuls of quinoa with some avocado slices.

Traditional snacks come into play more when I'm running around and need something portable, or when crunchy, salty cravings hit. Since I like having a stash on hand (and it's no added effort to make extras), I've scaled all the snack recipes to cups and quarts. The nuts, seeds, and popcorns here are also the sort of sharable snacks I put out as little nibbles when we have friends over. While my snacks haven't been tested for their bliss point, I can tell you the bowls are always emptied and everyone seems pretty damn happy.

SPICED PUMPKIN SEEDS MAKES 2 CUPS

In the world of portable protein-filled snacks, nuts get all the attention, but pumpkin seeds are an equally smart choice. I use hulled pumpkin seeds that I buy in bulk at the grocery store, but you can substitute seeds from a fresh pumpkin—the white shell is perfectly edible. A quarter cup of these will do you right when you need a spicy-sweet and crunchy snack. As a garnish, toss them on salads, soups, yogurt, or oatmeal. ■

Pumpkin seeds have a healthy dose of omega-3s and the immune system supporter zinc. They're also the only seed that is alkaline-forming.

2 cups raw hulled pumpkin seeds

1 teaspoon maple syrup

½ teaspoon fine sea salt

½ teaspoon ground ginger

½ teaspoon ground cinnamon

¼ teaspoon ground cloves

¼ teaspoon freshly grated nutmeg

1 Preheat the oven to 325°F. Line a baking sheet with parchment paper.

2 In a large bowl, toss together the seeds, maple syrup, salt, ginger, cinnamon, cloves, and nutmeg until they are evenly coated. Spread the seeds in a single layer on the lined baking sheet.

3 Bake, stirring every 10 minutes, until the seeds puff up and are lightly browned, about 25 minutes. Let them cool before storing in an airtight container.

EVERYTHING GOOD GRANOLA MAKES ABOUT 8 CUPS

Most commercially made granolas are sugar bombs full of corn syrup, highly refined oils, and questionable fillers—far from the virtuous food that the package leads us to think it is. Making your own is simple and more affordable, and allows you to control the type and amount of sweetener and oil. You also have the freedom to throw in whatever nuts, fruits, and seeds you like. In this version, I go with everything but the kitchen sink. The combination of three seeds with coconut flakes and cashews make it super-crunchy. I know granolas generally live among the breakfast foods in cookbooks, but it's more of a snack for me. I'll have a couple of handfuls to tide me over between meals, drop some into yogurt, or pack it up for traveling. ■

You can substitute regular honey, but it's worth looking for chestnut honey. It has a mildly nutty, almost savory, taste that gives the granola a complex, dark sweetness.

⅓ cup virgin coconut oil

1 teaspoon ground cinnamon

1 teaspoon ground ginger

2 tablespoons unsulfured blackstrap molasses

¼ cup maple syrup

2 tablespoons chestnut honey

4 cups old-fashioned rolled oats

¼ cup chia seeds

½ cup raw hulled pumpkin seeds

½ cup raw hulled sunflower seeds

1 cup raw cashews

1 cup unsweetened coconut flakes

Fine sea salt

½ cup dried cranberries

1 Preheat the oven to 275°F. Line 2 baking sheets with parchment paper.

2 In a small saucepan, combine the coconut oil, 2 tablespoons water, cinnamon, ginger, molasses, maple syrup, and honey and whisk over medium-low heat until everything is melted together, 3 to 5 minutes.

3 In a large bowl, combine the oats, chia seeds, pumpkin seeds, sunflower seeds, cashews, coconut flakes, and a couple of pinches of salt. Pour the wet ingredients over the oat mixture and stir until thoroughly combined.

4 Divide the granola between the baking sheets and spread in a thin, even layer. Bake for 30 minutes, then stir with a spatula. Continue baking until the oats are golden brown, 10 to 15 minutes longer. Let the granola cool completely on the baking sheets; it will harden and become crispy as it sits. Divide the dried cranberries between the two batches and toss to combine. Store in airtight containers at room temperature. (This also freezes like a champ.)

TROPICAL GRANOLA MAKES ABOUT 9 CUPS

I use virgin coconut oil in granola not only for its nutritional benefits, but for the warm, nutty, and lightly sweet flavor it brings. This granola has triple the coconut action—coconut oil, unsweetened coconut flakes, and coconut palm sugar—a rich, unrefined brown sugar with deep caramel flavor. ■

Large chunks of dried fruit lose their softness after being frozen and thawed, so if you plan to freeze this one, leave out the dried pineapple and papaya and toss those in once the granola is thawed and you're ready to eat it.

⅓ cup virgin coconut oil

1 teaspoon ground ginger

¼ cup honey

¼ cup coconut palm sugar

4½ cups old-fashioned rolled oats

½ cup hulled sunflower seeds

1 cup macadamia nuts, chopped

1 cup unsweetened coconut flakes

Fine sea salt

½ cup chopped dried pineapple

½ cup chopped dried papaya

½ cup banana chips, chopped

1 Preheat the oven to 275°F. Line 2 baking sheets with parchment paper.

2 In a small saucepan, combine the coconut oil, 2 tablespoons water, ginger, honey, and coconut sugar and whisk over medium-low heat until everything is melted and thoroughly combined, 3 to 5 minutes.

3 In a large bowl, combine the oats, sunflower seeds, macadamia nuts, coconut flakes, and a couple pinches of salt. Pour the wet ingredients over the oat mixture and toss until everything is well coated.

4 Divide the granola between the baking sheets and spread in a thin, even layer. Bake for 30 minutes, then stir with a spatula. Continue baking until the oats are golden brown, 10 to 15 minutes longer. Let the granola cool completely on the baking sheets. Divide the dried pineapple, papaya, and banana chips between the two batches and toss to combine. Store in airtight containers at room temperature.

CITRUS-SPIKED HAZELNUT AND ROSEMARY GRANOLA MAKES ABOUT 6 CUPS

Granola doesn't have to be a sidekick for yogurt or milk, and no one said it has to be sweet. I started playing around with savory granola at Hearth as a way to add textural contrast and an extra punch of flavor to vegetable dishes. I love this version with extra virgin olive oil, fresh rosemary, chestnut honey, hazelnuts, and citrus—familiar friends in Italian cooking. There's just enough sweetness for it to be at home in yogurt or milk, but rosemary's pinelike flavor and the full-bodied richness of olive oil earn this granola its place in salads, pureed soups, and anywhere else you would use croutons. ■

⅓ cup extra virgin olive oil

1 tablespoon chopped fresh rosemary

¼ cup chestnut honey

2 tablespoons unsulfured blackstrap molasses

4 cups old-fashioned rolled oats

¼ cup raw hulled sunflower seeds

¼ cup raw hulled pumpkin seeds

1 cup hazelnuts, halved

Grated zest of 1 lemon

Grated zest of 1 orange

Fine sea salt

¼ cup chopped pitted dates

¼ cup chopped dried figs

1 Preheat the oven to 275°F. Line 2 baking sheets with parchment paper.

2 In a small pot, whisk together the olive oil, 2 tablespoons water, rosemary, honey, and molasses. Cook over low-medium heat until the honey and molasses dissolve into the oil, 3 to 5 minutes.

3 In a large bowl, combine the oats, sunflower seeds, pumpkin seeds, hazelnuts, lemon zest, orange zest, and a couple of pinches of salt. Pour the wet ingredients over the oat mixture and toss until everything is well coated.

4 Divide the granola between the 2 baking sheets and spread in a thin, even layer. Bake for 30 minutes, then stir with a spatula. Continue baking until toasty brown, 10 to 15 minutes longer. Let it cool completely on the pans. Divide the dates and figs between the batches and toss to combine. Store in an airtight container at room temperature.

CURRY AND LIME CASHEWS MAKES 2 CUPS

Nuts are ideal for those late nights when I need a nibble after work. Thanks to their protein and healthy fats, it takes only a small amount to make me feel satisfied. It's almost too easy to go overboard on nuts, but these cashews have so much flavor from curry powder and fresh lime zest and lime juice that one handful really does the trick. I don't use additional oil or melted butter because nuts have a lot of oil of their own. ∎

Many ovens don't cook evenly, so it's important to shake the nuts around a few times while they roast. Pay special attention to the nuts near the edges of the pan since those tend to brown more quickly.

Grated zest of 1 lime
2 tablespoons fresh lime juice
4 teaspoons curry powder
1½ teaspoons fine sea salt
2 cups raw cashews

1 Preheat the oven to 300°F.

2 In a large bowl, combine the lime zest, lime juice, curry powder, and salt. Add the cashews and toss to coat.

3 Spread the nuts in an even layer on a baking sheet and roast, stirring every 10 minutes, until the cashews are lightly browned, about 30 minutes. Cool to room temperature, then store in an airtight container.

OLD BAY MARCONA ALMONDS MAKES 2 CUPS

Nothing good comes of drinking on an empty stomach, so have a handful of these spicy, smoky almonds during cocktail hour, or put them out at your next party. Marcona almonds are a Spanish variety that's rounder and fatter with a softer texture than the more common California almonds. Typically, they're packaged after they've been roasted in olive oil and salted. If you can't find them, substitute blanched almonds. ■

1½ teaspoons Old Bay seasoning

½ teaspoon Spanish smoked paprika

½ teaspoon fine sea salt

Juice of ½ lemon

1 teaspoon honey

2 cups Marcona almonds

1 Preheat the oven to 300°F.

2 In a large bowl, stir together the Old Bay, paprika, salt, lemon juice, and honey. Pour in the almonds and toss to coat.

3 Spread the nuts in an even layer on a baking sheet and roast, stirring every 10 minutes, until the almonds are toasted and fragrant, about 30 minutes. Cool to room temperature, then store in an airtight container.

SLOW-ROASTED MACADAMIA NUTS MAKES 2 CUPS

After Jeremy Fox, a friend and fantastic chef in California, cooked a guest dinner at Hearth, I found myself hoarding the leftover roasted macadamia nuts from one of his dishes. When slowly cooked at a low temperature, the nuts' buttery taste intensifies, they get crunchier and become sweeter and more caramelized than any macadamia nut I've ever had. I keep a jar of these around at all times now, and I often add cacao powder and a bit of orange zest for brightness and a hint of chocolate without any sugar. ■

2 cups macadamia nuts

1 tablespoon unsweetened raw cacao powder

Grated zest of 1 orange

Fine sea salt

1 Preheat the oven to 200°F. Spread the macadamia nuts on a baking sheet and roast for 2 hours, shaking them once halfway through cooking.

2 While the nuts are still warm, pour them into a large bowl and toss with the cacao powder, orange zest, and a couple of pinches of salt.

LEMON AND ROSEMARY POPCORN MAKES ABOUT 10 CUPS

Lemon and rosemary make magic wherever they're together, and popcorn is no exception. Dried rosemary is easier to grind into powder, but you can substitute fresh if that's what you have. If you're without a spice grinder or mortar and pestle, pile the dried herbs, garlic powder, salt, and lemon zest on a cutting board and finely chop them together. ∎

Movie theater and microwave versions aside, popcorn can be a stellar snack, especially for volume-eaters like me who appreciate a big bowl of food. Popcorn is high in fiber and polyphenols, a type of antioxidant.

1 tablespoon dried rosemary

1 teaspoon dried oregano

1 teaspoon garlic powder

1 teaspoon fine sea salt

Grated zest of 1 lemon

4 tablespoons extra virgin olive oil

½ cup organic popcorn kernels

Freshly ground black pepper

1 In a spice grinder or using a mortar and pestle, grind the rosemary, oregano, garlic powder, salt, and lemon zest into a powder.

2 In a large high-sided pot with a tight-fitting lid, heat 2 tablespoons of the olive oil over high heat. Drop in a couple of kernels. When those pop, add the rest of the kernels, cover, and shake the pot so the kernels get coated in oil. Continue shaking back and forth over the burner, holding the lid on until the popping slows down, 3 to 4 minutes.

3 Pour the popcorn into a large bowl and add the lemon-herb powder, a few grinds of black pepper, and the remaining 2 tablespoons olive oil. Use your hands to toss until all the ingredients are evenly distributed.

PECAN POWER BALLS MAKES 18 BALLS

The power of these tasty bite-size snacks is in the filling protein, quality fats, and fiber of the pecans, almonds, chia seeds, and flaxseeds packed into each one. I pop one, two at most, to hold me over for a few hours. They can also curb a mean sugar craving—the perfectly round, pecan-coated balls look a lot like the chocolate truffles you might get at a nice restaurant. There's a hint of pumpkin pie flavor happening too. Kids are usually more than happy to help make and eat these. ∎

Use a spice grinder or food processor to make ground pecans. The texture should be coarser than flour and similar to grains of sand.

Look for ground flaxseed (aka flaxseed meal) at your natural foods store or grind whole flaxseeds in a spice grinder. Your body can't digest the whole seed, so ground flaxseed is the best way to get the seeds' fiber and omega-3 benefits.

6 tablespoons ground pecans, plus ¼ cup finely chopped pecans

¼ cup ground flaxseed

2 tablespoons chia seeds

2 tablespoons maple syrup

½ teaspoon vanilla extract

2 tablespoons almond butter

Fine sea salt

1 In a bowl, combine the ground pecans, ground flaxseed, chia seeds, maple syrup, vanilla, almond butter, and a large pinch of salt. Using a rubber spatula, thoroughly mix together the wet and dry ingredients so they form a dough. Refrigerate for 15 minutes, or until the dough is firm but still pliable.

2 Spread the chopped pecans in a shallow bowl. Scoop out a heaping teaspoon of dough and, with wet hands, shape it into a ball. Roll it in the chopped pecans until fully coated. Repeat with the remaining dough, making sure your hands are wet as you roll. Store in an airtight container in the refrigerator for up to a week.

CACIO E PEPE POPCORN MAKES ABOUT 10 CUPS

Growing up, my sister and I were popcorn fiends. We popped it fresh, doused it in melted butter, and grabbed handful after handful while parked in front of the TV. Inspired by one of Italy's greatest pastas, *cacio e pepe,* I make a fresh-popped bowl of hot, crunchy popcorn lightly coated in salty cheese and the bite of freshly ground black pepper. If you're sharing with kids, you may want to portion out their servings before adding the black pepper. I do this for my daughter Stella, who is sensitive to all things spicy. This is easily doubled for a crowd or halved for a couple of people. ∎

As if the artificial flavor of store-bought microwave popcorn isn't bad enough, now there's "popcorn lung"—a type of lung cancer associated with chronic exposure to a chemical compound that adds artificial butter flavor to microwave popcorn. Heat from the microwave stirs up the compound, and it gets into the steam that people love to inhale when opening the bag. Do that enough over a long period of time and popcorn lung could be your future.

4 tablespoons extra virgin olive oil

½ cup organic popcorn kernels

½ cup freshly grated Pecorino Romano cheese

Fine sea salt and freshly ground black pepper

1 In a large high-sided pot with a tight-fitting lid, heat 2 tablespoons of the olive oil over high heat. Drop in a couple of kernels. When those pop, add the rest of the kernels, cover, and shake the pot so the kernels get coated in oil. Continue shaking back and forth over the burner until the popping slows down, 3 to 4 minutes.

2 Pour the hot popcorn (it needs to be hot or the cheese won't stick) into a large bowl and quickly add the Pecorino, the remaining 2 tablespoons olive oil, a pinch of salt, and a heavy shower of black pepper. Use your hands to toss everything together. Dig in immediately.

SWEETS

AS A RECOVERING SUGAR JUNKIE, I know eating sweets is a slippery slope. My relentless taste for sugar is as powerful as any craving for caffeine or nicotine and has led to some pretty hedonistic behavior. I started my sugar addiction early in life, nabbing Oreos, blueberry Pop-Tarts, and any sort of Entenmann's baked goods while at friends' houses (my mom never kept this stuff around). Pepperidge Farm Geneva cookies were a particularly good score—to this day, those buttery, chocolate-covered cookies are my kryptonite. At Hearth, I frequently caved based solely on the scent of fresh-baked cakes, cookies, or bread, and was all too fond of the small bowls of ice cream and sorbet constantly available in our pastry department. It was always nibbles here and there, so it never felt out of control (not counting the late-night sleeves of Chips Ahoy, which I considered an occasional "treat").

Years of this full-on sugar assault, paired with my overdosing on pasta and bread, inevitably led to crazy-high blood sugar and pre-diabetes. The harsh reality of having these issues is that I had to go to the extreme of quitting sugar cold turkey in order to reverse it. Besides the mindless bites of ice cream and cookies, that included ditching honey, maple syrup, and even some high-sugar fruits. I realized then just how much sugar dominated my diet. It found its way into everything, it seemed.

Now that my blood sugar is in check, sweets are back in my life. I find it unrealistic and unsustainable to maintain a ban on them forever. Sweets are a fundamental part of holidays, celebrations, and my career. I don't want to miss out on baking pies alongside my mom and my aunt at Thanksgiving or sharing in my daughters' birthday cakes. It seems like every important life event comes with a little bit of celebratory sugar.

Sentimental attachments aside, extreme food restrictions are notorious for backfiring. Everyone needs a little indulgence—you just have to be smart about it. I've wised up to the ways of thoughtful splurging, and it starts with the obvious: limiting processed sweets that pile on white flour, high fructose corn syrup, white sugar, agave syrup, and other types of highly refined sugars whose body-punishing effects go far beyond weight gain. Something remarkable happens when you ease up on these sugars. It's like hitting reset on your taste buds. You develop a sensitivity to sweetness and begin to notice the natural sugars in fruit and vegetables that never resonated on your palate before because it was dulled by excessive amounts of refined sweeteners.

As a result, I enjoy desserts a lot more when I control the quantity and quality of sugar (and flour, eggs, and milk) in them. I love the deeper, nuanced sweetness of natural sugars like honey, maple syrup, and coconut palm sugar. Coconut palm sugar is great because it's granulated and can be used cup for cup in place of white sugar. It gives another dimension of flavor to many of the desserts here, including Coconut Cacao Cardamom Panna Cotta (page 261) and Sweet Brown Rice Pudding (page 260). In place of all-purpose white flour, I often use whole-grain flours and nut meals, like the hazelnut meal that dials up the flavor in Hazelnut Brownies (page 256) and oat flour, which adds more chewy texture to Oatmeal and Dark Chocolate Cookies (page 258). If you don't have oat flour and you're in desperate need of cookies (hey, it happens), just buzz up rolled oats in a blender until they reach a coarse flour consistency. Works like a charm.

None of these upgrades will make dessert a healthy food essential to everyday life—that's not the point of dessert, anyway—but they do make sweet indulgences less taxing on your body. Most important, the desserts here taste as lusty and decadent and even more gratifying than their nutrient-bankrupt counterparts from store-bought dough logs or sacks of white flour and sugar. These sweets are an unapologetic pleasure.

SPICED APPLE, PEAR, AND CRANBERRY CRUMBLE SERVES 6

For a foolproof dessert, look no further than crumbles. They're simple, forgiving, adaptable to most fruits, and generally a dessert that everyone is excited to dig into. Most people want the serving that has a monstrous mound of topping, so I make sure no one gets shorted—this crumble is blanketed corner to corner with a crispy, honey-sweetened oat topping. This fall crumble is a sort of lazy man's apple pie. I prefer Honeycrisp or Gala apples and Bosc pears for this because they soften but still hold their shape. Leave the skin on the apples and pears—that's where a surprising amount of their fiber and nutrients are. ■

FILLING

2 cups cored, chopped Honeycrisp or Gala apples (about 2 large)

2 cups cored, chopped ripe Bosc pears (about 2 large)

1 cup dried cranberries

Grated zest of 1 lemon

1 teaspoon fresh lemon juice

2 tablespoons coconut palm sugar

TOPPING

½ cup chopped hazelnuts

1½ cups old-fashioned rolled oats

¼ cup virgin coconut oil

¼ cup honey

⅓ cup oat flour

½ teaspoon ground cinnamon

¼ teaspoon freshly grated nutmeg

¼ teaspoon ground cloves

¼ teaspoon ground cardamom

½ teaspoon ground ginger

Pinch of fine sea salt

1 Preheat the oven to 350°F.

2 For the filling: In a large bowl, toss together the apples, pears, dried cranberries, lemon zest, lemon juice, and coconut sugar. Spread the fruit in an 8 × 11-inch baking dish.

3 For the topping: In the same large bowl, stir together all the topping ingredients to combine. Evenly distribute the oat topping over the fruit.

4 Bake until the oats are lightly toasted and the fruit is bubbling around the edges, about 35 minutes. Let it sit for 10 minutes before serving to allow the topping to get crispier.

YOUR BODY ON SUGAR

Remember when the only downside of eating too much sugar was getting cavities? It seems laughable now that sugar has been exposed as the reason that many people's health is in the toilet. After realizing that the low-fat craze only made people fatter, studies focused more on simple carbohydrates, especially sugar (which is pumped into many low-fat products to mask their cardboard taste). The results: Eating too much sugar makes us fat, destroys our livers, and opens the doors to type 2 diabetes and heart disease. If you're tempted to pretend it's not true, I'm with you. But sugar's negative effects are no joke, and you have to consider how much play sugar is getting in your diet if you expect to fit into your pants and have a body that actually works in 10 years.

You may be thinking you're home free because you don't eat candy and cookies, but if you slam back sodas, bottled flavored teas, or fruit juice with any regularity, you're basically mainlining sugar. One 12-ounce soda has a whopping 10 teaspoons of sugar. Sugar is also hidden in fast food and practically every processed food on the shelves—ketchup, jars of tomato sauce, peanut butter, even supposed healthy products like yogurt, instant oatmeal, and energy bars. And it's not just sugar. All refined carbs—including white bread, many crackers and pastries—act like sugar in the body, so those count too. The food industry relies on it so heavily that the only way to avoid overeating sugar is to cut out nearly all processed foods and drinks.

Most of the sugar I ate was in the form of bread, cookies, pasta, and hamburger buns—all high on the glycemic index and impossible for me to pass up. I would joke that they were like crack . . . which science now supports as a legit fact. Sugar is addictive, lighting up the same feel-good areas of the brain as cocaine and morphine. It's why just one cookie or one bite of ice cream didn't satisfy me—it took increasingly larger hits for me to get the sugar rush. The problem is that our bodies aren't built to handle the mountains of sugar we're pouring into them. Compounding this is the fact that sugar fuels your appetite like gasoline fuels a fire: The more sugar you eat, the more you crave. The good news is that the opposite is also true: The less sugar you eat, the more sensitive you become to it, and the less you need.

When you eat a piece of chocolate cake, the carbs are broken down into glucose—the sugar your body uses for energy—and then sent into your bloodstream. Your pancreas responds by releasing insulin, which lowers blood sugar levels by sending the glucose to cells for energy and then to your liver. Normally, the amount of insulin released is just enough to bring things back to an even keel. But if you're putting cake, soda, or any refined carb in your face regularly, an increasing amount of insulin has to be released to deal with all that sugar. This uptick in insulin triggers hunger, making you head back for more cake. If you do this often, your body can't possibly use as much energy (glucose) as you're putting in, and insulin may direct it to be stored as fat.

Fructose, the sugar in fruit, acts a little differently than glucose. It is abosrbed by your liver, so fructose doesn't spike blood sugar levels and is relatively low on the glycemic index. Sounds like the holy grail of sugar, right? It is, if you're getting fructose only from whole fruit, where it exists in relatively small amounts and is packaged with fiber. But if you're eating highly processed packaged foods, you're likely getting a ton of high fructose corn syrup or the bullshit "healthy" sweetener, agave syrup, which has a freakish amount of fructose (about 97 percent). These concentrated forms of fructose put a heavy load on your liver, which can store only so much sugar. When your liver is full, the sugar gets converted to fat. So eating sugar, especially fructose, too often and in large amounts ultimately results in weight gain and serious wear and tear on your liver that can lead to fatty liver disease.

To your body, it doesn't matter if it's a Pop-Tart or a fancy baguette, white sugar or honey: All forms of sugar can lead to some nasty outcomes if you down too much. That being said, some sources of sugar are better than others. (See my guide to sweeteners and how often to indulge in them, page 252.) Fruit and naturally occurring sweeteners are the best options. High-quality maple syrup tapped out of a tree and honey from local bees are a lot less processed than granulated sugar and high fructose corn syrup (which clearly had a very long road from a stalk of corn or sugarcane). Read the labels of the natural sweeteners you buy to make sure they're unadulterated versions—some may have added refined sugars. And despite the fact that sugar substitutes like Splenda, NutraSweet, and Sweet'N Low don't raise blood sugar levels, I don't use them. They're heavily

processed and still relatively new to the food world, so their long-term health consequences are unknown. Also, most are hundreds of times sweeter than table sugar, so they keep your palate accustomed to overly sweet foods.

After my doctor-prescribed hiatus from sugar, I found that I didn't crave it as much. And when I started indulging in it again, I realized that it didn't take much to satisfy my urge. When I took my kids to the chocolate shop L.A. Burdick for hot chocolate one afternoon a few years ago, I was completely satisfied with a 2-ounce Dixie cup portion. They have insanely good, high-quality hot chocolate, but I still couldn't believe that tiny portion was enough for me. It was such a victory.

SUGAR: THE GOOD, THE OKAY, AND THE DON'T GO THERE

SWEETENER	WHAT IS IT?	NUTRITION NOTES
MY GO-TOS		
Honey (preferably raw)	Produced by honey bees from the nectar of various flowers	Dark honeys like buckwheat and chestnut have more antioxidants.
Maple syrup	Boiled-down maple tree sap	A good source of antioxidants and minerals, especially zinc and manganese. I use Grade A, which is lighter and easiest to find.
Granulated coconut palm sugar	Boiled-down nectar of coconut palm trees	Has a deep caramel flavor, can be used cup for cup in place of granulated or brown sugar. It's lower on the glycemic index than cane sugar.
Molasses	A thick, dark syrup made by processing sugarcane or sugar beets into table sugar	Unsulfured varieties are best. Blackstrap molasses is the thickest, most nutritious variety because of its high mineral content.
USE SPARINGLY		
Organic cane sugar (aka evaporated cane juice)	A golden granulated sugar extracted from sugar cane	Slightly less refined than regular sugar.
Organic brown sugar	White sugar with a bit of molasses added to it	Organic guarantees it's from pesticide-free sugarcane.
Stevia	Sugar substitute extracted from the stevia plant	Has no effect on blood sugar levels, but it's 300 times sweeter than regular table sugar. Some brands have added sugars, so read the labels.
AVOID		
Agave syrup	Made from the juice of blue agave cactus	Highly processed and has an incredibly high concentration of fructose.
High fructose corn syrup	Corn syrup processed with chemicals to convert some of its glucose to fructose	Sweeter and cheaper than sugar, a manufacturers' choice for processed foods. It has more fructose than regular sugar and triggers a stronger insulin response.
Aspartame (NutraSweet, Equal), sucralose (Splenda), and saccharin (Sweet'N Low)	Man-made artificial sweeteners	Used in diet sodas and low-fat products because they don't raise blood sugar levels. They're as far as you can get from whole, real food.

OLIVE OIL CAKE SERVES 10

When it comes to adding rich flavor to cakes, butter isn't the only game in town. Olive oil makes an incredibly moist, soft cake that's traditionally brightened up with fresh citrus zest. The flavor of the olive oil you use will really shine through, so make sure it's a good one that has the soft, fruity qualities that are typical in Southern Italy, rather than the peppery Tuscan oils that I love for just about everything else. Think of it as the Italian version of a pound cake, as good on its own as it is topped with seasonal fruit. ■

1¼ cups extra virgin olive oil, plus more for the pan

1¼ cups whole wheat flour, plus more for the pan

1 cup coconut palm sugar

3 large eggs

1 cup honey

1 teaspoon vanilla extract

Grated zest of 1 lemon

Grated zest of 1 orange

1 cup almond flour

½ teaspoon baking soda

½ teaspoon baking powder

Pinch of fine sea salt

1 Preheat the oven to 325°F. Lightly coat a standard-size Bundt pan with olive oil and flour. Tap out the excess.

2 In a large bowl, beat together the coconut sugar, eggs, and honey. Add the olive oil, vanilla, lemon zest, and orange zest, and mix well.

3 In a separate bowl, whisk together the whole wheat flour, almond flour, baking soda, baking powder, and salt. Add the dry ingredients to the wet mixture and whisk until just combined.

4 Pour the batter into the pan and bake until the edges are browned and pulling away from the sides, about 1 hour. Let the cake cool in the pan for 15 minutes before inverting it onto a serving plate.

MIXED BERRY CRUMBLE SERVES 6

With all the natural sweetness of summer berries, you don't need much additional sugar to make this a seriously delicious dessert. Expect a good amount of berry juice to accumulate in the bottom of the pan. I spoon some of that saucy sweetness along with each serving. ■

FILLING

½ pint strawberries, hulled and quartered (about 2 cups)

½ pint blackberries (about 1½ cups)

1 pint blueberries (about 2½ cups)

Grated zest of 1 lemon

1 teaspoon fresh lemon juice

2 tablespoons coconut palm sugar

TOPPING

½ cup chopped walnuts

1½ cups old-fashioned rolled oats

¼ cup virgin coconut oil

¼ cup honey

⅓ cup oat flour

½ teaspoon ground cinnamon

Pinch of fine sea salt

1 Preheat the oven to 350°F.

2 For the filling: In a large bowl, toss the berries with the lemon zest, lemon juice, and coconut sugar. Spread the berry mixture in an 8 × 11-inch baking dish.

3 For the topping: In the same large bowl, stir together all the topping ingredients to combine. Evenly distribute the oat topping over the berries.

4 Bake until the oats are lightly toasted and the fruit is bubbling around the edges, about 35 minutes. Let it sit for 10 minutes before serving, so the berries cool and the topping gets crispier.

HAZELNUT BROWNIES MAKES 16 BROWNIES

Brownies from a boxed mix are high on my list of nostalgic desserts, but their jarringly sweet, artificial taste doesn't do it for me anymore. Straddling the line between cakelike and fudgy, these brownies have a deep, dark richness and a light, moist crumb (a rarity among gluten-free desserts). All the best brownies have nuts, so I use chopped nuts and hazelnut meal here. Nut meals—whole nuts ground into a coarse flour—add texture, protein, and fiber and have a moist quality that works very well in baked goods. I use Bob's Red Mill hazelnut meal, but you can also grind hazelnuts in a good food processor. Almond meal is a good substitute. ∎

As an alternative to the microwave, you can melt the chocolate and coconut oil together in a metal bowl set over a pot of simmering water. Just make sure the bottom of the bowl doesn't touch the water.

½ cup virgin coconut oil, plus more for the pan

5 ounces dark chocolate (70% cacao), chopped

½ cup light brown sugar

½ cup coconut palm sugar

½ cup hazelnut meal

¼ cup oat flour

¼ teaspoon baking soda

Fine sea salt

2 extra-large eggs

1 tablespoon pure vanilla extract

½ cup chopped toasted hazelnuts

¼ cup unsweetened coconut flakes, chopped

1 Preheat the oven to 350°F. Lightly grease an 8 × 8-inch baking pan with coconut oil.

2 Melt the chocolate and coconut oil together in the microwave in 30-second intervals, stirring with a rubber spatula between each interval, until the chocolate is completely melted and smooth.

3 In a large bowl, mix together the light brown sugar, coconut sugar, hazelnut meal, oat flour, baking soda, and a pinch of salt.

4 In a separate bowl, beat the eggs with the vanilla. Add the egg mixture to the bowl of dry ingredients and stir until the batter is smooth (there is no gluten, so overworking the batter is not a concern). Pour the chocolate-coconut oil mixture into the batter and stir until everything is thoroughly combined. Fold in the toasted hazelnuts and coconut flakes so they're evenly distributed throughout the batter.

5 Pour the batter into the pan and bake until the edges are firm and a toothpick inserted in the center comes out with a few moist crumbs, about 35 minutes. Let the brownies cool completely in the pan before cutting.

PEANUT BUTTER CACAO NIB COOKIES
MAKES ABOUT 2 DOZEN COOKIES

Cacao nibs are coarsely ground cacao beans, and I toss them in anywhere I want crunch and the deep, bittersweet flavor of really dark chocolate— yogurt, fruit, granolas, and good ol' soft and chewy peanut butter cookies. They're full of flavonoids, which have antioxidant powers, and they make a great way to get a chocolate fix without added sugar. ■

½ cup creamy peanut butter

½ cup honey

½ cup coconut palm sugar

½ cup virgin coconut oil

1 large egg

1 teaspoon pure vanilla extract

1 cup whole wheat flour

3 tablespoons ground flaxseed

½ teaspoon baking soda

½ teaspoon baking powder

Pinch of fine sea salt

¼ cup cacao nibs

1 Preheat the oven to 350°F. Line 2 baking sheets with parchment paper.

2 In a bowl, combine the peanut butter, honey, sugar, and coconut oil using a rubber spatula. Add the egg and vanilla and mix until smooth.

3 In a separate large bowl, whisk together the flour, ground flaxseed, baking soda, baking powder, and salt. Add the flour mixture to the bowl of wet ingredients and mix until just combined. Stir in the cacao nibs.

4 Scoop out tablespoons of dough and roll each one into a ball (wet hands makes this easier). Arrange them on the baking sheets about 2 inches apart. Dip a fork in water, shake off the excess, and lightly press down on the center of each dough ball with the back of the fork. Repeat at a 90-degree angle to create a grid on top of the dough.

5 Bake until the cookies are golden brown on the edges, about 12 minutes. Transfer to a rack to cool.

OATMEAL AND DARK CHOCOLATE COOKIES MAKES 2 DOZEN COOKIES

These stunners are exceptionally chewy and crammed with pockets of melted dark chocolate. Spelt and oat flours give the cookies character, making them hearty and satisfying without weighing them down. These aren't delicate cookies, so if you're in a rush or buried in dirty dishes, mix everything in one bowl, rather than mixing the wet ingredients separately from the dry and then combining. This may be violating some baking laws, but it turns out fine for me. ■

Spelt flour has more protein and fiber than whole wheat flour and can be substituted cup for cup. It has a low level of gluten, so some people find it easier to digest.

1½ cups spelt flour

1 cup oat flour

2 cups old-fashioned rolled oats

1 teaspoon baking soda

Pinch of fine sea salt

1 cup sliced almonds

1½ cups dark chocolate chunks (70% cacao)

2 extra-large eggs

¾ cup coconut palm sugar

¼ cup unsulfured blackstrap molasses

1 cup virgin coconut oil

1 tablespoon pure vanilla extract

1 Preheat the oven to 350°F. Line 2 baking sheets with parchment paper.

2 In a large bowl, stir together the spelt flour, oat flour, rolled oats, baking soda, salt, almonds, and dark chocolate.

3 In another bowl, whisk together the eggs, coconut sugar, molasses, coconut oil, and vanilla. Add the wet mixture to the bowl of dry ingredients and stir until just combined.

4 Portion the dough into heaping tablespoon-size balls and arrange them on the lined baking sheets, about 2 inches apart. Bake until the edges are beginning to brown, about 15 minutes. Let them cool for 2 minutes, then transfer the cookies to a rack to cool for a few more minutes before grabby hands get to them.

SWEET BROWN RICE PUDDING SERVES 6 TO 8

If you're looking for a soothing, creamy bowl of comfort—the mac 'n' cheese of desserts—this is it. I'm always amazed at the amount of creamy starch that comes out of sweet brown rice; it lends itself perfectly to rice pudding. Coconut and hemp milks add rich flavor and next-level creaminess, while cinnamon and cardamom give the pudding a little exotic warmth. It's altogether addictive. ∎

To help give the pudding body, I prefer moderately creamy hemp milk to the thin consistency of almond and rice milks.

1½ cups sweet brown rice

1 cinnamon stick

1 (13.5-ounce) can full-fat unsweetened coconut milk

1½ cups hemp milk

Finely grated zest of 1 orange

½ teaspoon ground ginger

¼ teaspoon ground cardamom

¼ teaspoon ground cinnamon

¼ teaspoon freshly grated nutmeg

½ cup coconut palm sugar

Fine sea salt

1 vanilla bean

1 In a large pot, combine the rice, cinnamon stick, and 3 cups water and bring to a boil over high heat. Reduce the heat, cover, and simmer for 30 minutes. Take it off the heat and let it sit covered.

2 In a separate pot over medium heat, combine the coconut milk, hemp milk, orange zest, ginger, cardamom, cinnamon, nutmeg, coconut sugar, and a large pinch of salt and whisk together. Split the vanilla bean in half lengthwise and scrape the seeds out and add them to the pot along with the bean pod. Bring to a boil slowly over medium-high heat. As soon as it comes to a low boil, reduce the heat to medium-low and simmer for 10 minutes. Remove the vanilla bean pod.

3 Remove the cinnamon stick from the pot of cooked rice and add the rice to the spiced milk. Increase the heat to medium and cook, stirring occasionally, until the pudding has thickened, but still has a bit of liquid, about 10 minutes.

COCONUT CACAO CARDAMOM PANNA COTTA SERVES 4

I wave the panna cotta flag high, and not just because it's an incredibly simple, classic Italian dessert. Its biggest asset is a silky smooth texture that feels remarkably luxurious and light. Panna cotta is also a chameleon that can take on the flavor of any seasonal fruit, sweet spices, and whole milk you like. I use coconut milk instead of the traditional heavy cream—it's every bit as thick and rich. ■

1 packet (2¼ teaspoons) unflavored powdered gelatin

1 (13.5-ounce) can whole unsweetened coconut milk

1 teaspoon ground cardamom

3 tablespoons unsweetened raw cacao powder

3 tablespoons coconut palm sugar

Fine sea salt

1 In a small bowl, sprinkle the gelatin over 3 tablespoons cold water and let it sit for 5 to 10 minutes to dissolve.

2 In a 2-quart saucepan, combine the coconut milk, cardamom, cacao powder, coconut sugar, and a pinch of salt. Cook over low heat until the sugar is dissolved, about 5 minutes. Turn off the heat, add the gelatin mixture, and whisk until it's completely dissolved. Pour through a fine-mesh sieve into a large bowl or a vessel with a spout.

3 Divide the mixture evenly among 4 (4-ounce) ramekins, cover with plastic wrap, and transfer to the refrigerator to set for at least 2 hours and up to overnight.

BLUEBERRY PIE SERVES 8

I'm drawn to simple, rustic, shareable sweets—the kind I can make with my daughters and set in the center of the table with a stack of plates and forks. The pinnacle for me? Pie. When my family descends on Martha's Vineyard for summer vacation, it's a pie-making, pie-eating frenzy. Rhubarb, strawberry, and, my favorite, blueberry pie. The point here is to highlight the blueberries—no frills, no unnecessary steps, and no added sugar needed. Since it requires very few ingredients, this pie relies heavily on fresh summer blueberries and good-quality grass-fed butter. For me, there is no crust except an all-butter crust. I'm willing to switch up the flour though, and I've found whole wheat pastry flour produces an equally flaky, mild, and buttery crust as white flour. ∎

Cold ingredients are key to tender, flaky crust. Make sure your butter is well chilled and your water is ice-cold. Also, it helps to chill your pastry cutter and metal bowl in the freezer and pull them out only when you're ready to make the dough.

CRUST
14 tablespoons (1¾ sticks) unsalted grass-fed butter

2 cups whole wheat pastry flour, plus more for rolling out

½ teaspoon fine sea salt

FILLING
6 cups blueberries (about 3 pints)

Finely grated zest of 1 lemon

1 tablespoon fresh lemon juice

3 tablespoons cornstarch

Pinch of fine sea salt

1 For the crust: Cut the butter into pats, lay them on a plate, and freeze them for 15 minutes.

2 In a large metal bowl, whisk the flour and salt together. Scatter the frozen pats of butter in the flour. Using a pastry cutter or a fork, work the butter into the flour until it resembles coarse crumbs with pea-size pellets of butter visible throughout. Drizzle in ½ cup very cold water. Use your hands to gather the dough together, but handling it as little as is needed to get it into one mound. As soon as it comes together (when you can pinch a piece of it and it holds its shape), dump out the dough onto a clean work surface and shape it into a fat cylinder, like a can.

3 Separate one-third of the dough, so you have 2 mounds. Shape each mound into a flattened round disk, wrap them tightly in plastic wrap, and refrigerate for at least 1 hour and up to 3 days. The dough can also be frozen for up to 1 month.

4 Preheat the oven to 425°F. Position a rack in the center of the oven and place a foil-lined baking sheet on a lower rack to catch any blueberry juice overflow from the pie.

5 Remove the larger disk of dough from the refrigerator. On a well-floured surface, flatten the dough and sprinkle a bit of flour over the top and on a rolling pin. Roll the dough out into a round roughly 12 inches in diameter. Picture a clock and roll from the center out toward every number, all the way around. Each time the dough expands about an inch around, sprinkle a bit more flour, flip the dough and roll out the other side. Use a pastry scraper around the edges to make sure the dough isn't sticking. (It's okay if the edges crack—they can be pinched together.) Fold the dough in half, then in half again. Put it in the center of a 9-inch glass pie plate, unfold it so it's centered, and gently press it into the edges. The dough should

hang about an inch over the rim of the pan.

6 For the filling: In a large bowl, combine the blueberries, lemon zest, lemon juice, cornstarch, and salt and toss to coat. Pile the blueberries into the pie crust (they should almost overflow).

7 Remove the remaining disk of dough from the refrigerator and roll it out into a round about 10 inches in diameter using the same method as before. Fold it in half, then in half again, lay it over the top of the blueberry mound and unfold it. Working your way around the edge of the pie, press the top and bottom crusts together and fold them under. Crimp the edges with your fingers to seal. Using a paring knife, cut 4 (3-inch) slits in the top crust and 4 shorter slits in between those, so steam can escape.

8 Put the pie on the center rack in the oven and bake for 20 minutes. Reduce the heat to 350°F and bake until the crust is golden brown and the blueberries are bubbling, about 40 minutes longer. Let it cool on a wire rack for at least 1 hour. The pie will thicken the longer it cools.

People have such anxiety about making pie. *Relax*. Making dough can actually be quite zenlike, especially when doing it by hand. The only way to learn what good pie dough should look and feel like is through the tactile sensation of hand-forming it. With a food processor, it's too easy to overwork the dough and overmix the butter—two actions that kill the potential for good crust.

BLUEBERRY PIE (PAGE 262)

READING AND RESOURCES

BOOKS

The Great Cholesterol Myth by Jonny Bowden and Stephen Sinatra

The New Glucose Revolution by Dr. Jennie Brand-Miller, Dr. Thomas M. S. Wolever, Kaye Foster-Powell, and Dr. Stephen Colagiuri

The Inflammation Syndrome by Jack Challem

Nourishing Traditions by Sally Fallon and Mary Enig

The 4-Hour Body by Timothy Ferriss

The Blood Sugar Solution by Dr. Mark Hyman

Clean by Dr. Alejandro Junger

Fat Chance by Dr. Robert Lustig

In Defense of Food, Food Rules, and *Cooked* by Michael Pollan

Why We Get Fat by Gary Taubes

WEBSITES

Monterey Bay Seafood Watch: SeafoodWatch.org

Eat Wild: EatWild.org

American Grass-fed Association: AmericanGrassfed.org

Local Harvest: LocalHarvest.org

ACKNOWLEDGMENTS

My acknowledgments begin with my wife, Amanda. Why and how does my wife play so integrally into the reality of this book? Well, if it weren't for her, I would probably still be a smoking, boozing, carb-loading, unhealthy mess, and the chances of me writing a book about what it means to have a good food day would be zero. She got me on the train to wellness, and her influence never came in a nagging, preaching kind of way; it was delivered consistently, over time, with a level of nonchalance that somehow had a tremendous impact. All the time I looked and felt like shit, I coexisted with my svelte, energetic, beautiful wife, and kept thinking, *I want some of what she's got*. Up early, eating a great breakfast, exercising, doing yoga, packing delicious-looking salads for her lunch and cooking simple, clean proteins with some local veggies for dinner. She understands the power of what we put in and on our bodies and advocated for getting all the toxic shit out of our apartment, insisting on organic or local meat and produce. My wife, more than anyone I know, cares deeply about the food she eats and feeds to our two beautiful daughters, and for that, I am eternally grateful. She is also an English teacher and has poured over page after page of the many iterations of this book from conception to completion, lending her expertise and insights along the way. The title of this book and the name of my first restaurant are both Amanda's doing, and all of this together just scratches the surface of why I am grateful to have her as my partner in crime.

Tammy Walker, damn . . . what can I say? Talk about doing a lot of the heavy lifting. Without her dedication this book would still be a work in progress. We spent countless afternoons together cooking and talking and eating, and cooking some more. In the process, she acquired an uncanny ability to capture my thoughts and beliefs on the pages of this book. Incredibly generous with her time, she has been a genuine, positive, and smiling presence throughout this process, and a *huge* part of why this book came out as great as it has. Michael Harlan Turkell was a joy to work with as well, and his photos speak for themselves. I enjoyed my days working with him so much that I seriously contemplated a career change to food stylist.

Close to four years ago, Pam Krauss was willing to sit in a nondescript midtown coffee shop, drinking crappy coffee and listening to me pitch this book. She believed in the idea of a chef-driven companion cookbook to all of the health and nutrition books that I was devouring, and thankfully she supported this project from the get-go. The fact that she did means a whole lot—she is a no-bullshit kind of lady and I respect that immensely.

Jessica Freeman-Slade and the entire crew at Clarkson Potter, you guys rock! Jessica awed me time and time again with her thoughtfulness and attention to detail. She is whip-smart and I am lucky to have had her as my editor.

Tim Ferriss's *4-Hour Body* was one of the first books I devoured on the subject of living a better life. (Confession: I originally thought of *A Good Food Day* as a companion cookbook to *The 4-Hour Body,* although Tim might not be down with pasta recipes.) Tim is the ultimate badass, always pushing and experimenting with ways to optimize time, health, and wellness. He has taught me and his readers how to be cleaner and leaner, and I am grateful to have the ability to shoot him a text to ask about the newest source of glutathione or what have you. He's a busy guy who somehow always finds the time to help.

While we are on the topic of badasses, I've got to mention David Black, agent extraordinaire. I've always felt safe with him in my corner—he was such a strong advocate for me over the years, and I am honored to be on his roster of authors. The miniature hand-painted rocking chairs with which he gifted each of my daughters when they were just weeks old are indicative of the fact that behind his hard-assed business savvy is a man with a huge, thoughtful heart.

Last, and very important, I want to thank my mom for instilling in me a love of food and everything that surrounds the rituals of eating. She was way ahead of her time: "Eat real food, not too much, mostly plants" was her MO decades before Michael Pollan gave eloquent expression to such an approach. Growing her own vegetables on our property in Milton, New York, she taught me the beauty and wonderful taste of quality ingredients, prepared simply. When she cooks me something to eat, it feeds me like nothing else in the world can. All I can say is, You are an amazing mama, Mamma.

INDEX